Ahong

2018

Theory SE

Leadership Tripod

A NEW MODEL FOR EFFECTIVE LEADERSHIP

SECOND EDITION
Now includes:

- Expanded Text
- Case Studies
- Discussion Questions
- Self-Reflection Exercises

Dr. Al Long

Leadership Tripod

Al Long

ISBN 0-9748391-1-6 (previously ISBN 1-929478-42-9)

Power Publishing
13680 N. Duncan Drive
Camby, IN 46113

This book is manufactured in the United States of America.

Library of Congress Cataloging in Publication Data in Progress.

Published by Power Publishing
13680 N. Duncan Drive
Camby, IN 46113

Editor: Debbie DeWitt

DEDICATION

This book is dedicated to Vince Myer, a man who cares about those he leads. His life illustrates in teaching and personal example the essence of true Shepherd Leadership.

A PERSONAL NOTE

In my life I have been very blessed to have observed and served under some very effective leaders. While some were Theory X leaders, they were effective in their individual situations and sometimes exhibited aspects of other leadership theories as well.

Vince Myer, the man to whom this book is dedicated, has always been and continues to be a Theory SE leader, something you will learn more about in this book.

I have had the privilege of knowing, observing, and being under the leadership of Vince for most of my life. He started out as my baseball coach when I was ten years old. Instead of driving us relentlessly as some coaches do, he shepherded us with compassion and love. I am totally convinced that I would not be where I am today had it not been for Vince's selfless example of leadership. You see, Vince cared about those he led.

Of the many times he intervened on my behalf, one example stands out. Growing up in Advance, Indiana, I was the poor kid from the unpainted house on Wall Street. Believe me, Wall Street in Advance, Indiana during my childhood wasn't anything like the Wall Street of today's evening news. Vince knew my home situation and never treated me as less important or worthy of his attention than any other kid. Others certainly knew how to "rub it in," but not Vince. As a matter of fact, he wanted to be sure I had the same opportunities others had.

You see, Vince cared about those he led.

On one evening during my sophomore year in high school, Vince showed me how much he cared. I held a job, but happened to take that evening off to play basketball at open gym. Vince was now my basketball coach. Taking me aside where no one else could hear us, he asked me if I needed shoes. I ducked my head in embarrassment and shuffled my feet. Then I finally answered yes because, of course, I did need new shoes. He proceeded to tell me to go to the local sporting goods store and pick up a pair he had already paid for.

That gesture of kindness is a lesson I've never forgotten. Taking a personal interest in those he coached and reinforcing their sense of self-worth are ways that Vince cared for those he led. Thanks, Vince!

It is my hope that this book will encourage others to be the kind of leader Vince Myer was and showed me how to be.

Dr. Al Long

ACKNOWLEDGEMENTS

There are many people who contributed either directly or indirectly to the writing of this book. It would be impossible to thank each person who helped, but some deserve mention and acknowledgement for their contributions to the manuscript.

My wife is by far the single most important person in my life. She has supported me throughout my career and continues to do so in this stage of my life. She gives balance to our life together and is the perfect example of what the reader will be introduced to in the text when reading about a healthy culture. Her behaviors and beliefs are always in tune. Her steadfast faith and work ethic is an inspiration to me and others she touches on a daily basis.

The rest of my immediate family also deserves mention. They are always a source of inspiration and support for my efforts. Tad, Brad and Chad, our sons, but also my best friends, are men, I can go to in times of need and know they will give me straight answers and help me keep my priorities straight. Their wives Cathy, Dee and Kathy are also like daughters and daily make our sons even better men on a daily basis. Our grandchildren; Abby, Tyler, Victoria, Trevor, Trey, Deacon, Jaxon, Olivia and Maxwell make each day special as we watch them grow and mature.

My mother, Dorothy, deserves credit for instilling in me a strong work ethic and a goal-oriented personality. My dad, Darol, without whose influence made me who I am today, also deserves credit.

And finally, to Joe and Mary, my in-laws, I give them credit for being Shepherd leaders.

Mom, Dad and Joe are now gone, but certainly not forgotten and still have daily influence on my life and the lives of our family and extended family on a daily basis.

INTRODUCTION

Another book on leadership? That's just what we need, isn't it? Another author telling us everything we're doing wrong, then magically providing the answers to our leadership problems. A prescription; a new program; a new panacea for all leaders. That's not what this book is all about.

Coming from a background that includes extensive leadership experience in the fields of business and education, I know enough to say there are no easy, magical solutions to leadership problems. This book is the culmination of several years of study, observation, and personal leadership experience. It also includes valuable input about solving leadership problems from colleagues and friends in a variety of occupational settings.

While many books have been written and continue to be written about leadership, few give a real-life application model to judge whether or not effective leadership is taking place in any given situation. *Leadership Tripod* is designed as a practical approach to studying leadership and identifying the characteristics of effective leadership. The *Leadership Tripod* concept was developed as a visual model to help organizations evaluate progress toward more effective leadership. The tripod model gives organizations and organizational leaders something substantive to compare to what is actually happening within their organizational culture. Like a surveyor's or photographer's tripod, the *Leadership Tripod* has legs and braces. These are the leadership elements or principles we will examine in this text. Further, the *Leadership Tripod* rests upon a base, and just as a functional tripod must be on a level base before it can be used properly, the *Leadership Tripod* must have a firm foundation.

Within this book the reader will examine not only the conceptual framework of the tripod's individual elements and principles, but will also study real-life examples of these principles. The reader will also assess various organizations' successful and unsuccessful attempts to implement the model. Along the way, we will discuss traditional leadership theories, as well as introduce the reader to an additional leadership theory.

Each chapter ends with a self-assessment, allowing the reader to evaluate his or her current status and where that individual would prefer to be instead. These assessments are designed not only for the individual's improvement, but also for the improvement of the organization and a metacognitive reflection of what needs still exist.

In this second edition of the *Tripod*, we have added case studies as well as discussion questions to enable the reader to use the book in continuous development activities within an organization as well as for use in the university setting.

In helping the reader better understand what effective leadership is and is not, *Leadership Tripod* targets:

- Leaders—of corporations, organizations, businesses, etc.
- Those who lead or train leaders
- Those under leadership

As you can readily see, this target readership involves everyone, because each of us falls into one or more of these categories. At different stages of our lives, we may be both leader and led, trainer and trainee. Most important, we all have room for improvement.

As I sit on the balcony of a beautiful condo in Bonita Springs, Florida, I can't help but relate leadership to the sight before me. The beautiful ocean is like one of the alluring leadership positions I have been offered over the years in business and education. The ocean is powerful and full of possibility, just like many of the leadership positions I have undertaken. But the ocean is also untamed and relentless, continually pounding the shore much like leaders in any type setting can and are pounded on a daily basis.

Leadership carries with it heavy burdens of responsibility. As leaders, we are like the solid rocks on the shore, attempting— sometimes in vain—to hold back the ocean, trying to protect the shore from the never-ending onslaught of waves, trying to calm the fears and meet the needs of the organizations we lead. Like the rocks on the beach, the harsh reality is that leadership can only withstand the pounding of the surf if it is securely anchored to a firm foundation.

The *Leadership Tripod* cannot totally control the ocean, but it can serve as a model to help equip the leader and his or her organization with foundational principles, assuring that the ocean won't wash the sand from under the rocks. It is not that elusive panacea, but it can be a strong levy to help the leader and the organization better withstand the turbulent waters of today's fast-paced, sometimes cutthroat world.

Let us begin our journey in *Leadership Tripod* by examining the structure of the tripod, seeing how each element contributes to overall effectiveness in leadership. Later, we will look at additional tools to fine-tune the fundamentals. Throughout our study we will evaluate the responsibilities of those who select and support leaders to see what their roles are as well. All of this should contribute to a solid model for studying and evaluating leaders and leadership.

My hope is that after reading *Leadership Tripod*—whether as a leader, one who is under leadership, or as one who is responsible for the selection and support of leaders—you will better understand what true leadership is and how to effectively apply proven leadership principles to every aspect of your professional and personal life as well.

To develop more and more principled leaders and organizations is a primary reason this book is written. Until we have leaders and organizations more concerned about principles than pay checks, we will not be where we need to be and our organizations will not be as strong as they can and should be. Leaders or future leaders without strong knowledge, skills and dispositions in leadership are like the young man in the following parable:

Parable of the Would Be Artist

Once upon a time there was a young man who aspired to be an artist. He had seen a movie of a famous master and thought being an artist is what he wanted to be his life's work. He went about gathering supplies from any place he could find them, not worrying about their age or condition.

He first found an old painter's pallet that had long since lost all its colors, but that didn't bother the young man because he had found some black and white paint in the garage. He had also found an old tripod that had long been abandoned by a highway crew, but yet he thought it would work well enough to suit his purposes. He had also gone down to the local dump and found an old tent from which he proceeded to cut a piece of canvas for his soon to be masterpiece. After all, the artist in the movie had made it look so easy to create those beautiful pictures.

Just in case the painting thing didn't work out, however, the young man had a secondary plan. He decided that if painting wasn't his bag, surely taking breathtaking photographs would be an easy task. He could use the tripod for either goal. He could either attach his tent canvas for painting or he could mount his camera on the top to capture the beauty of nature he so longingly wanted to copy.

The eager young man gathered his new found treasures and headed off into the forest to capture nature at its most beautiful. While the young man's intentions were good, his tools and knowledge were not. As he arrived at the most beautiful place in the forest he stopped and looked around. He thought this would be the perfect place to create his masterpiece. He set up his tripod, attached his tent canvas, opened his black and white paint and began to create his representation of nature.

He was quickly dismayed and disappointed because the canvas tent would not accept the paint and even the small amounts that did stick to the surface were only black and white and did not capture the beauty of the forest or the now quickly setting sun.

Not to be defeated, the young man pulled out his camera thinking he could quickly attach it to the top of the tripod and he could be the artist he wanted to be through the medium of photography. The problems immediately became apparent, however, when he attached the camera and found that the tripod was not level. Thinking this could be easily fixed, he adjusted one leg of the tripod, but when that was level, another leg began to slowly sink into the soft floor of the forest.

Thinking he could still capture the beauty of the moment, he tried holding the tripod, with the camera mounted on top while and looking through the viewfinder all at the same time. The problem was, of course, he could not get the picture he desired by trying to utilize the unsteady tripod.

This young man who had the best of intentions. He had the desire to perform, and he had the vision of what he wanted to accomplish. However, he did not have the tools or training to be the artist he wanted to be. Defeated and dejected, he abandoned his flawed tools, picked up his trusty old camera and went slinking back through the beautiful forest without having captured any of the magnificence of nature or experiencing any joy in his journey. The young man was not an artist.

The moral of this parable and the significance for the book you are about to read are:

Your pallet needs to be filled with multi-colored paints.
Your canvas needs to be clear and ready to accept the paint.
You must continue to create.

Your tripod needs to be level, standing on solid ground with braces to hold it steady.

All of this will become clear as you read the pages of *Leadership Tripod*.

CONTENTS

PRE-ASSESSMENT

Note to the reader: take the time to complete this assessment before you read further.

In order to measure improvement, one must know where to begin. This pre-assessment instrument is provided to give the reader a base of reference or knowledge starting point. A post-assessment instrument is included at the end of this book, intended to measure the impact of what you have read. Those of you who are highly competitive or who get anxious when taking any kind of "test," relax.

There are no right or wrong answers. These assessment instruments are designed simply to give you an idea of your knowledge base regarding the topic of leadership—before and after reading *Leadership Tripod*.

1. What is your level of knowledge in leadership theory and application?

5	4	3	2	1
High	Moderate	Neutral	Some	None

2. Are each group's job and/or leadership responsibilities clearly stated in your organization?

5	4	3	2	1
High	Moderate	Neutral	Some	None

3. Do you know exactly what is expected of you?

5	4	3	2	1
High	Moderate	Neutral	Some	None

4. Do you have the authority to allow you to clearly carry out your responsibilities?

5	4	3	2	1
High	Moderate	Neutral	Some	None

5. Are accountability systems clearly established for you and other groups?

5	4	3	2	1
High	Moderate	Neutral	Some	None

6. Is there a strategic plan in place and is it clearly understood and used as a base of reference for decisions?

5	4	3	2	1
High	Moderate	Neutral	Some	None

7. How would you rate the communication lines within your organization?

5	4	3	2	1
High	Moderate	Neutral	Some	None

8. How would you rate your ability to communicate?

5	4	3	2	1
High	Moderate	Neutral	Some	None

9. Are the organization's ethics and morals clearly stated and evident?

5	4	3	2	1
High	Moderate	Neutral	Some	None

10. Are your ethics and morals clearly evident?

5	4	3	2	1
High	Moderate	Neutral	Some	None

11. Is the culture (climate) of the organization healthy and do your behaviors and beliefs match that of the organization as a whole?

5	4	3	2	1
High	Moderate	Neutral	Some	None

12. How important do you think the concept of leadership is to the success of your organization?

5	4	3	2	1
High	Moderate	Neutral	Some	None

Total Score: _____

CHAPTER 1

LEADERSHIP
A LOOK AT LEADERSHIP THEORIES

A Look at Leadership Theories

As we begin this journey of the second edition of *Leadership Tripod*, I am no longer in Florida overlooking the ocean where I wrote the first edition. I am now in Las Vegas overlooking the "City of Lights". As I write, I can't help but think of the tremendous task of leading an organization like Caesar's Palace. As I gaze out my window I can't help but notice that just the magnitude of the building would make a leader shudder at the enormity of the task of overseeing and leading such an organization. Just the sheer numbers of staff, buildings and dollars it takes to keep the casino going is an enormous undertaking. Some leaders could look at this as an undoable undertaking, others as an energizing leadership challenge. Either way, *leaders must not let the enormity of the task rob them of the joy of the journey*.

In today's society it seems the art of leadership is losing its luster and many who in the past would have taken the leadership journey are choosing to let others lead. This author believes one reason for this shift away from leadership is the lack of study and understanding of what leadership is and the failure to recognize the rewards that come from being a successful leader.

Rewards at Caesars are always going to be extrinsic—like the money a player might win at the tables or on the slots. Likewise, leaders can and do receive extrinsic rewards in the form of higher salaries. Too often today, however, people are deciding the extra salary is not worth the extra work and responsibility of leadership. This is again, I believe, because of a lack of knowledge about leading and the lack of focus on the other type of rewards—intrinsic rewards. An intrinsic reward is the feeling of satisfaction of successfully leading a company to higher levels of success. This is a reward no one can describe. You have to experience it!

We must make leadership a viable, real craft or art and help others understand that there are more rewards than money that come from being a leader. The jackpot the leaders hit in any successful leadership experience is not just the coins or tokens kicked out of the slot machine, but it is also the internal feeling of satisfaction that a difficult task has been and is continuing to be accomplished. You can't feed those feelings back into the slot or you can't buy groceries with intrinsic rewards, but these rewards can keep you going back again and again to difficult leadership decisions to enhance the organization you lead. The 360-degree feedback you receive when someone you lead acknowledges that your leadership made a difference in their lives is one of the most satisfying feelings one can experience. It is even better than opening a special gift on Christmas.

The question then becomes, how do we lead more successfully and how do we convince others to join in the leadership journey? The answer is to study the craft, and gain the knowledge, skills and dispositions needed to become successful leaders.

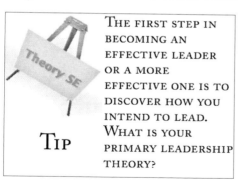

THE FIRST STEP IN BECOMING AN EFFECTIVE LEADER OR A MORE EFFECTIVE ONE IS TO DISCOVER HOW YOU INTEND TO LEAD. WHAT IS YOUR PRIMARY LEADERSHIP THEORY?

TIP

In recent decades, countless books and studies have focused on leadership. The fact that leadership is essential for personal and organizational growth is undisputed. *How* leadership is best cultivated and facilitated, however, is the subject of much debate. This chapter will briefly survey various leadership theories, identifying key concepts and seeing how they relate to the top piece of our leadership tripod.

Trait Leadership Theory

Trait Leadership Theory is one of the earliest leadership theories, originating in the early part of the twentieth century. The basis of Trait Leadership Theory assumes that by studying certain very effective leaders, one could identify and categorize specific leadership traits. Leadership traits were first studied in a military context. However, it didn't take long for those hiring leaders in the nonmilitary sector to adapt the essential principles to their context. The basis for this theory is to try to predict success by matching a specific leadership trait to a leadership candidate for an identified leadership position.

The thought behind this theory was that if successful leaders could be studied and specific traits could be identified, when a leadership position opened those searching for a new leader could simply identify the traits they desired and the search for a candidate who possessed those traits.

Although simplistic at first glance, in some applications the theory seemed to work. An example would be during the Vietnam War. I have been told that when the war was at its most intense level, draftees were singled out for specific tasks based on experiences and traits they possessed. For example, soldiers from the Midwest were selected to be point men on squads because they had learned the trait of shooting by instinct. The army had learned through experience that soldiers from the Midwest grew up hunting game and would shoot first and think later. This was a trait soldiers from other parts of the country did not possess. Soldiers from other parts of the country seemed to analyze the target and this analysis time could be deadly. The Midwest soldier had the instinct (trait) developed in the hunting fields of firing quickly so the target did not escape.

This trait was ample reason for the Army to put these young men in positions of leadership. Without leaders with this trait, many more soldiers could have lost their lives in the jungles of Viet Nam. Can this trait of quick response also apply in some businesses today? Of course, the answer is yes. Some organizations may need a leader who knows how to make quick, decisive decisions to keep the company viable, but other organizations may need the more analytical leader to make the organization successful.

The Right Fit

In looking at another example of how Trait Leadership Theory might apply today, let's look at someone who is being considered for a leadership role in a weight loss company. If one candidate overeats and is obviously overweight, he or she probably will not be the best "fit" for the position—metaphorically speaking. Further, if this leadership candidate does not truly believe in the importance of healthy eating habits and physical fitness, he or she will undoubtedly have a tough time leading the organization and "selling" the idea that weight loss is important. Thus, those reviewing candidates for this position would be looking for the *trait* of discipline in a candidate's physical life.

Profiling Key Traits

Recently a university was looking for a new dean for its graduate school of business and education. In the initial meeting of the leadership team, members were asked what they would look for as they reviewed candidates for the position of dean. Team members immediately began to profile the ideal candidate, listing characteristics they saw as important to this leadership role. Among several things mentioned were that the dean should be open, cooperative, and experienced. The members of this college leadership team were actually beginning to identify *traits* they felt were essential in order for the dean to successfully lead the college.

At first glance the "modern" student of leadership theory might quickly dismiss the Leadership Trait Theory as too simplistic and even passé. However, Trait Leadership Theory has continuing value even in contemporary society.

The problem is in relying *only* on **traits** in selecting a leader. A physically fit candidate for the weight loss clinic might possess the trait of personal discipline, but still have poor managerial and leadership skills. The college dean might be open and cooperative, but be unable to prioritize his appointments. Although traits play an important role, leadership is more than the sum of traits.

As a person who has hired leaders, I wish I could tell you I have never made the mistake of relying too heavily on the traits of a prospective leader when filling a vacancy. That is not true. I can speak from experience when I say that when those placing leaders rely too heavily on traits in the absence of other qualities the results can be disastrous for the organization and the leader who was improperly placed.

In one particular fiasco where a leader was chosen only on the basis of he right traits, everyone worked hard to overcome what seemed to be a mistake from the beginning. It took a great deal of time to try and fix a non-repairable problem. Finally, after a few months of misery for all concerned I brought the person in and we agreed we should sever our working relationship. I would love to state it was totally the unsuccessful leader's problem, but that is not true. Those of us who were responsible for bringing this person into our organization were just way too simplistic and superficial in our analysis of the needs of the leadership position.

Behavior Leadership Theory

Looking beyond traits as the primary criteria for identifying leaders, the Behavior Leadership Theory switched the focus to the behaviors of effective leaders. This theory essentially involved comprehensively analyzing the behaviors of effective leaders, and then identifying which behaviors are most responsible for success in leading others. Candidates matching those patterns of behavior were seen as the most likely to fill a leadership position successfully. The Behavior Leadership Theory also lent itself readily to organizational adaptation; i.e., properly interpreted, certain behaviors could be taught to leadership trainees.

Like Trait Leadership Theory, this theory is simplistic, but Behavior Leadership Theory can't just be dismissed. There are certain behaviors those searching for leaders of their organizations are, and should be, looking for. Those looking for leaders and leaders themselves just can't think that behaviors are the ONLY thing to look for. Behavior Leadership traits provides information we need to help make informed decisions, but it is too simplistic to make crucial leadership decisions only on observed or desired behaviors.

Later I will discuss Knowledge Leadership as a painter's pallet. All theories and knowledge goes on the pallet to be placed on the canvas, but if we only paint with one color our portrait of leadership will be simple, shallow and without application to many leadership situations.

A Real Life Example

In March, while watching the NCAA men's and women's basketball tournaments, and thinking about Behavior Leadership theory and how a leader and an organization could error in placing too much emphasis on the Behavior Leadership Theory, a certain coach came to mind. This coach's behavior on the bench and with the press was classically authoritarian, yelling and driving his players to succeed. They did succeed. They were perennial winners and regularly made trips to the "big dance".

While this coach's behavior of total control and domination did drive several fine athletes away, those who stayed were highly successful in the win-loss column of sports.

The problems began to surface, however, when this coach's behaviors that were so canonized on the court began to have him vilified off the court. His behaviors never changed from one setting to another. Where they were acceptable when winning a game, they weren't acceptable when trying to "drive" the college administration to his way of thought about how to handle various situations. When his behavior carried even into his dealing with the public, the administration of the college finally came to the decision that they could not continue to support his leadership of the team. The behavior traits that caused this coach to be so successful, were the very traits that led to his demise. The coach's palette had only one color on it and that is how he always led.

Which Behavior is "Right"?

Looking back to our example of using the Trait Leadership Theory in selecting a leader at the weight loss clinic, let us look at how using the Behavior Theory in choosing the leader would work. The human resources director might look for a leader whose behaviors coincide with the mission or current needs of the company. Such behaviors might include physical fitness and a daily workout regimen, as well as dedication to the company and a history of staying with a company for an extended period of time. If the weight loss clinic were experiencing financial difficulties or personnel problems, they might target someone able to "clean up" the company. In this case, the weight loss clinic would want a leader with a proven history—someone whose past behaviors included the ability to streamline the workforce by fostering cross-training and eliminating unproductive or superfluous employees.

Similarly, the college searching for a new dean might look for behaviors such as team development and the ability to delegate responsibility to his or her directors. The leadership committee might also want the dean to lead by modeling the behaviors they felt were important. These could range from actually teaching classes and meeting regularly with all faculty and staff, to expecting the dean to belong to a certain church denomination, attend athletic events, and join service clubs.

Qualifying Effectiveness

The Behavior Leadership Theory by itself can be problematic and lead to somewhat simplistic decisions. Even though it can be used as a guide to help profile what the decision-makers are looking for in a leader, this theory cannot guarantee that identifying certain behaviors will necessarily produce a good leader. No leadership position can be studied in totality, assuring that all behaviors are categorized and then taught and/or learned and that continually displaying the same behavior in every situation will result in effective leadership.

The weight loss clinic could hire a leader based on behavior criteria and still not resolve their financial issues. The new college dean could demonstrate all the applicable behaviors and fail at helping the college meet its mission. Conversely, the dean could demonstrate none or very few of the desired behaviors and still be a very effective leader.

Traits and behaviors are important building blocks in constructing an ideal leadership candidate, but they do not comprise the entire person, nor answer all the needs of the organization.

Situational Leadership Theory

The Situational Leadership Theory developed by Hersey and Blanchard defines an effective leader as one who leads according to how the situation dictates.[1] An extrapolation of this theory would suggest that a person who leads one way in one situation would not necessarily lead the same way in the next. The theory basis is that the leader leads as the situation dictates.

Consistently Inconsistent: An example of Situational Leadership

I have been blessed to have met Coach John Wooden on several occasions and listened to him speak several times. I once heard him relate what I believe to be a great example of Situational Leadership.

He said that many coaches and organizations error by believing that everyone should be treated (led) consistently. He said people need to be treated "consistently inconsistent". He meant that they should be led by the way the situation dictates.

He gave the example of having two players of equal ability and skill. One works hard in practice and one does not. In a game they make the same mistake. Does the coach handle both players the same? Wooden's answer is no! You treat them consistently inconsistent because if you treat them the same, the message to the player who has worked hard is that his hard work has done him no good because he is treated the same as the one who has contributed less.

The same could be true of leadership in any organization. If two members of a leadership team or manufacturing team show different levels of commitment to the organization, they too should be treated differently as the situation dictates.

Of course these are simplistic examples and one could quickly see how this theory can be applied to not only matters of personnel, but also to market trends, economic conditions, etc.

I personally believe this idea can be expanded to a Positional Situational Leadership theory as well. The premise is based on a belief that a person may be an effective leader placed in the proper leadership situation. An extrapolation of this thought would be that a leader could be highly ineffective in one leadership position and be highly effective in a different situation.

Short-Term or Short-Sighted?

Given the two scenarios we have been using, let us first apply this theory to the weight loss clinic. The positional situational theorist would say that even though our overweight leadership candidate might not be a "fit" for the clinic, he or she might make an excellent leader for a crisis intervention center, where weight is not the key issue.

Positional Situational Theory also points to circumstance as affecting outcome. For example, a leader might seem to achieve great success by increasing membership and bringing the clinic into financial stability. However, if there has been a recent upswing in the area's population—most notably, an increase in the number of health-conscious residents—the leader more likely may have benefited from favorable circumstances rather than leadership expertise.

Positional Situational leadership is evident today when corporations in trouble bring in a leader to "turn the company around." Decision-makers and corporate boards allow this kind of shake-up because of the difficult situation in which they find themselves. There's a sense that the new leader will be effective because he or she will only be there for a short time.

The error in this thinking is precisely its short-term focus. Effective leadership isn't measured by someone's ability to swoop in and make dramatic changes that temporarily affect the bottom line. That line on the chart may rise sharply, but most likely, it will descend again just as quickly.

Short-term decisions often have long-term consequences that are not examined through the lens of Situational Leadership Theory. For example, perhaps the new leader advocates eliminating all of computer-illiterate employees and hiring only those with computer savvy. As a result of the "shake-up," did the company lose some valuable and loyal employees? Do the new computer-literate employees lack depth and experience? Might the company have avoided this collateral damage by offering its employees computer training instead?

McGregor's Theories - More Paint on the Palette

In studying how leaders lead, Douglas McGregor categorized them into two camps: Theory X and Theory Y.[2]

Theory X Leadership

According to McGregor, the Theory X leader basically believes that those he or she is leading inherently want to do the very *least* expected of them. The Theory X leader believes all employees need to be watched carefully and driven hard, or the work won't get done. If left on their own, the "workers" will take from the organization, doing as little work as possible and getting away with as much as they can. Theory X leaders have people working *for* them rather than *with* them. The term micromanager is usually associated with a Theory X leader.

An organization and those responsible for selecting leaders can be Theory X in nature as well. In this kind of organization, the leader is required to show "heads rolling" in order to prove "effective" leadership. Unfortunately, when problems come, the organization and the leadership will look for people to blame instead of problems to solve.

Defining Success

Ironically, many Theory X organizations are viewed as highly successful. I held a leadership position not long ago in an organization that believes in Theory X leadership. When going through the selection process, it was apparent to me that the organization had long believed in Theory Xing its staff and leaders. This was totally contrary to my style, but the organization's board adamantly professed a desire to change the way they had been leading. They said they wanted a leader with a very different style, one capable of taking them from where they had been and leading them in a new direction. They sincerely seemed committed to this change, even though their peers in the corporate world viewed them as highly successful just the way they were.

The problem came when I actually started trying to go in a new direction. The board had been used to micromanaging for so long that when I didn't follow that style, they couldn't adapt to the change. They felt that if they were not privy to all decisions and if people weren't constantly being targeted for dismissal, then progress was not taking place. They *talked* about change, but it was soon evident to me that they were not comfortable with change.

As a leader with a different leadership style, I might have quickly jumped to the conclusion that I was right and they were wrong. However, the fact remains that this organization was capable of meeting its goals without a change in leadership style. The reason this organization was meeting its goals without changing the leadership style is explained in our original discussion of Positional Situational Leadership Theory. In this particular situation, as I learned firsthand, Theory X leadership was probably adequate for this particular organization.

Soon after I left, the stakeholders of the organization realized, partly because of my quick departure, that the organization was not as healthy as had been portrayed by the Board. A majority of the sitting Board was defeated in the next election and a new majority came on to attempt to change the culture to a more cooperative atmosphere and rid the organization of the "micro-management" mentality.

Again one cannot dismiss Theory X as being wrong and not of any benefit. The exact opposite is true. There are times in organizations where anything other than Theory X might lead to disaster.

The military is an example of an organization that has to be led primarily with a Theory X mentality. This leadership style is not necessarily because leaders believe soldiers are incompetent, but because orders need to be followed without question or discussion.

Likewise, effective leaders must at times be Theory X leaders, even though it may not be the way they normally lead or want to lead. There are times when it is necessary to direct, inspect, and redirect in order not to lose a potentially excellent person, account or opportunity.

Theory Y Leadership

McGregor's second theory is called Theory Y. This is the antithesis of Theory X. Theory Y leaders believe that those they work *with* inherently want to do the very best they can for themselves and their companies. Left to themselves, the associates will work hard and share a sense of accomplishment when their company succeeds. Theory Y leaders believe their job is to do everything they can to assure that those who work with them have all the tools and resources they need to be successful. If the workers are not successful, Theory Y leaders will first look at themselves to see if they have failed to provide the environment necessary for achievement. Rather than blame people for underachievement, they examine the system or the root problem. Whereas the Theory X leader faults *people* for failure, the Theory Y leader faults the *process*.

Steady as She Goes

Those who know me would probably tag me as a Theory Y leader. I recently led an organization which could also be characterized as a Theory Y organization. It took years for this organization to make the transition from Theory X to Theory Y. The difference between this organization and the previously mentioned Theory X organization is that the board which hired me had carefully planned a logical transition to a Theory Y mentality. Everyone was committed to the change, so the change was implemented successfully—even though it didn't happen overnight.

The very fact that change takes time is a primary reason why organizations and individuals many times give up and fall back to the way they have operated in the past. Our human nature is to revert to behaviors with which we are most familiar and comfortable. If an individual leader or an organization has for years led in a Theory X manner, it will take time, effort and a great deal of study and training to get stakeholders to think and act differently.

It would be great if we could just wave a magic wand over our staff, boards, customers, ourselves and any other stakeholders and make the changes we would like to see implemented to improve our organizations, but that is just not the case.

Although the process of change in the organization mentioned before took years to totally be reformed, the working climate was improved from the very beginning of the transition. It just took several years to totally bring the change into place.

One specific step necessary to bring about change was through comprehensive strategic planning which will be discussed later in the book.

As an example of how this planning can parlay an organization into utilizing Theory Y Leadership style, let's look at an example of a planning session. In this case, all stakeholders involved come to the realization that staff serving clients in the most direct way do not feel supported or adequately trained. The Theory Y leader would gather members of staff and receive input in how to re-align or restructure the process so that front line staff could feel valued and be equipped to do their jobs. The Theory Y leader's goal would be to enable and equip the staff to achieve success.

Theory Z Leadership

William G. Ouchi originated a leadership style labeled Theory Z.[3] Its similarity to McGregor's Theory Y lies in Ouchi's belief that people do want to achieve success both for themselves and for their companies. How this success occurs and the roles of the leaders in helping people achieve success is what differentiates Theory Z from Theory Y.

Whereas McGregor would say that the leaders should make the success of the workers their primary task, Ouchi suggests that the leader should create an environment in which teams work together for the success of all. Leaders would be responsible for fostering joint decision-making and cross-functional teams. The atmosphere would be one of cooperation and shared decision-making, as well as shared accountability. Rather than having the leader decide what needs to be in place in order for the workers and the organization to achieve success, it would be up to all stakeholders to jointly analyze and decide the best direction and structure so all could achieve maximum success.

Applying Theory Z

Organizing teams and allowing these teams to decide the direction of the organization may not work in every situation. But many manufacturing firms are finding the Theory Z leadership model extremely viable. Where previously many such companies were organized in a highly mechanistic, bureaucratic manner, the ever-changing nature of manufacturing today frequently necessitates quick decisions at the basic floor level if firms are to remain competitive. This involves decentralized decision making; i.e., bypassing the cumbersome "chain of command" that can slow or paralyze production. Many Japanese companies, especially in the technology sector, follow this organic model, readily lending themselves to Theory Z leaders and leadership.

In the past few years since the first edition of *Leadership Tripod* was written, I have been fortunate to have become involved with a company and leaders who live out Theory Z out on a daily basis. Because of this and the success we have had, my family has started another business modeling the "Z" mentality we witnessed (along with SE as you will learn later).

Part from necessity and part from philosophy the owners of this company have involved and continue to involve nearly all stakeholders in the decisions affecting the success of the company. From customers to sales to service to manufacturing, input is cultivated and decisions made at every level without fear of reprimand. Because of this, the company has more than doubled its business in each of the last two years. The company remains nimble, flexible and profitable by creating and celebrating a Theory Z culture.

Sorting It Out

What then should a leader do when faced with a leadership position that does not coincide with his or her leadership style? There really are not many good alternatives. To avoid this kind of situation, leaders and those selecting leaders need to do a thorough job of prescreening candidates for compatible styles. Still, even a thorough prescreening cannot guarantee the ideal candidate for the organization, or prevent unforeseen circumstances from changing the original criteria. Mismatches can occur (see the appendix for sample interview questions). Faced with such a mismatch, there are only two options: 1) the organization can make the appropriate changes to adjust itself to the leader's style, or 2) the leader can find a different position. Both of these options can be stressful to all involved, but not nearly as stressful as conflicting ideologies about how to effectively lead an organization that continue to occur month after month.

Many examples have taken place in recent years where the leader and the organization are at odds as to the leadership needed to move a company or organization to the next level of excellence. This happens in all sorts of situations whether it be a long established company or a not for profit philanthropic venture. The real problem comes when both the leader and the board or directors have such battles both publicly and privately that the organization and those stakeholders within the organization suffer. This win-lose or lose-win mentality has nothing but detrimental effects on all involved.

It is during these times of conflict when calmer minds must prevail and a win-win solution found. An example of how leaders with a vision for the organization rather than themselves took place recently in the world of athletics. A head coach who had served as the leader of a very successful program had a less than stellar season. This coach also just happened to be within one year of fulfilling his contractual agreement with the university as well as being at an age where retirement was a possibility. When those in the decision making position made it known they felt a need for a change of leadership, the coach first looked at options at other universities, but ultimately worked out a win-win solution by cooperating with the university administration and then being involved in the placement of his successor as a co-head coach for the remaining year of his contract. This cooperative solution caused the coach, the players, the university and the new leader all to participate in a win-win solution to a difficult transition time from one leader to another.

Although this cooperative spirit and attitude is by far the best for all concerned, it does not always happen this way. In the not too distant past, the newspapers were full of stories where the head of a major Hollywood studio was forced from his leadership position by stockholders and the Board of Directors. The organization suffered from bad publicity as well as lower stock prices because of the very public display of conflict between leadership and the stockholders. Both sides and the stockholders lost. The stock will rebound, but the damage to organizations's image and stakeholders within the organization will take time to repair as will the culture.

In times of conflict and change in leadership philosophy,

calm minds and emotions need to prevail and ramifications of actions and non-actions need to be taken into account. Both sides of the conflict must think through the issues and get the feelings and emotions in a secondary position rather than foremost in the decision making process. This is not to say emotions aren't an important factor, but they should not be the driving factor in the decision making process of change in leadership.

Theory S Leadership

I propose still another Leadership theory: Theory S. The S stands for Shepherd. As I have studied leadership over the years, I've looked for the ideal model to embody the finest in leadership principles. The shepherd seems to best exemplify that ideal model. I envision two subdivisions to my shepherd model. SW leadership represents a Western culture shepherd. SE leadership represents an Eastern culture shepherd.

Fostering a Relationship: The Eastern Shepherd

Recently, my wife and I had the opportunity to visit Israel, where modern-day culture rubs elbows with ancient ways and traditions. While visiting a tell in Samaria, we saw a shepherd tending his flock much as shepherds have done for hundreds of years. There was a sense of tranquility in the scene before us. Even more, it seemed that the shepherd and his flock were comfortable together and that the sheep completely trusted the shepherd. What was striking was the evident caring and pride the shepherd had for his sheep. Some of the ladies and gentlemen in our group made comments about a cute young lamb in the flock. The joy and pride on the shepherd's face when he heard these comments showed how he sincerely cared for his sheep. What a lesson this was to me about how we should all care for those we lead. If we could capture the same desire in our leadership to care for those we lead as the shepherd cared for his sheep, there would most certainly be a reciprocal caring of those being led to the leader and the organization he/she leads.

While doing a bit more detailed study on the Eastern culture shepherd, we also learned that in the Eastern culture a shepherd creates a summer sheepfold each evening and leads his flock into its protection for the night. As the sheep pass individually through a small opening, the shepherd puts his staff or rod across the opening. He does this to check each animal for injuries and overall stamina since they have been in open pasture all day. After seeing to their needs, applying medicinal ointments if necessary, and determining that they are safe, he then lies down across the small opening—effectively presenting himself as a barrier to any predators or thieves that might try to enter the sheepfold.

Once again the Eastern culture shepherd has given us a Leadership model we could follow with the ones we strive to lead. Wouldn't it be wonderful if leaders could have only a portion of the caring of the shepherd? According to this model, a leader would periodically check those he/she leads for issues or problems they may be facing. Not necessarily in their personal lives (although this author thinks that could at times be appropriate also), but in their professional lives and their attempts to make the organization they work for successful. If the leader would systematically and intentionally make deposits into the lives of those being led, times of trouble and conflict would most assuredly have less of an impact impeding the success of all stakeholders involved.

Driving the Flock: The Western Shepherd

Shepherds of the Western culture tend their flocks very differently from what we observed in Israel. The Western shepherd "drives" the flock, generally using a dog to nip at the sheep and herd them where the shepherd wants them to go. The shepherd/sheep relationship is different, too. When the shepherd yells at the sheep, they move—not because they want to, but because they fear their shepherd. There is no long-term relationship between the sheep and shepherd. In fact, it's a one-way relationship, all for the benefit of the shepherd. In Western culture, sheep are a commodity and are essentially raised for wool and meat. That's a win-lose situation—the shepherd wins and the sheep ultimately lose.

Theory SW Leadership

How does all this relate to leadership? Let's look at the owner of a restaurant. The food is good and the place is always busy. The owner and his family are well known in the community and thought to be one of the wealthiest families in the county, maybe even in the state. So why am I choosing this organization as an example of Theory SW Leadership?

The reason is the way he treats his employees. The community is full of disgruntled past employees. You see, this leader believes the workers are there only to serve his needs. If they fail to do that or if they make any kind of mistake, they are out! This restaurant owner leads by intimidation; the "dogs" that nip at the heels of his employees are his managers, usually other family members who share in the profits of the business. Further, this leader pays minimum wage, using the most downtrodden to his benefit, and then callously discards them. His philosophy is that there is always someone in need of a job, so he gets what he can from his workers, then replaces them when they no longer meet his needs.

This "shepherd" doesn't care to know his sheep and his sheep definitely don't know him. If they knew beforehand what they were in for, they probably would never agree to work for him. Some work because they have no place else to work. If this is the case, they most assuredly will be gone to a new place of business and a new shepherd at the very first opportunity they have.

Theory SE Leadership

Let's replace the current owner of the successful restaurant with a Theory SE Leader, one who leads the way an Eastern shepherd would lead. An Eastern culture leader (SE) would care individually about his or her workers and attempt to run the business in a way that would benefit all. This leader believes in the workers and feels an obligation to make their lives better. This is not to say the SE leader or owner abhors financial success! Not at all. But the driving force or motivation for making the business profitable is to include the workers in the success. The relationship between owner and workers is long term, leading to mutual celebrations of longevity. There is no need to "drive" the employees to do their work. Instead, the SE leader examines different ways to ensure employee happiness and success. Many times I have found these SE leaders to have a heartfelt desire for their employees to share in the profits of the company.

The SE Leader should not mistakenly be labeled as a business wimp or one who is careless about making money. What I have found in my cursory study is just the opposite. Many times these leaders many times are self-made men and women who know business well and know equally well how to succeed. What they do not have in common with the SW Leader is the idea that workers are just another commodity. They share with other SE Leaders a belief that a successful business is successful *because of* the workers, not *in spite of* them.

The company our family has launched is striving to be an SE company. We have a philosophy that all will benefit from any success the company may enjoy. To exemplify this we have set up a structure so that all our staff will benefit financially as the company grows and we will <u>not</u> limit what anyone can earn. The more successful the company is, the more successful our flock will be.

We also make sure we take the time to know one another and all those we serve. We are trying to live the model of SE and develop long-term win-win relationships with both our internal and external customers.

It's Not Just a Job

Several months ago, I did a strategic planning seminar for a Theory SE leader. I didn't know this was an SE leader until he told me what he hoped to gain from the seminar. His goal obviously wasn't the "bottom line," because he shut down his business and made the necessary arrangements for all his employees to attend. He simply wanted to learn about strategic planning *with* his staff so they could all achieve success and feel a sense of "ownership" in the success of the business.

I can just hear some of you who are reading this right now! "You've got to be kidding," you might exclaim. "No business owner would even *think* that way, much less make it happen!" Well, if that is what you are thinking, you probably are operating from a Theory SW mind-set. Unlike some other business owners I've known, this owner sincerely wanted to help the company grow and increase its profit margin so those working for him (*with* him, he would say) could reap some of the benefits.

I don't want to leave the impression that he didn't want to make money in the process; he just wanted to make sure that all involved in the company's success benefited from that success. His belief was and continues to be this: if employees can see a chance to share in the growth and success of the company, they will work to ensure the company's success. In the process, they enjoy their work and don't regard it as "just a job."

As evidence of the owner's sincerity in arranging for the seminar, by the end of the day the owner and employees had adopted a specific objective—the creation of a profit-sharing plan to be implemented within the first six months of the upcoming year.

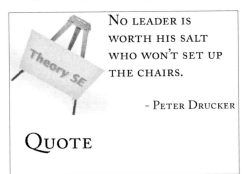

No leader is worth his salt who won't set up the chairs.

- Peter Drucker

Quote

It was also interesting during the day to observe the close-knit relationship these individuals shared with one another. Not that they were alike in many ways, but it was evident that they cared about one another—not just at work, but outside work as well. They talked about hockey, soccer, vacations, kids, and ailing family members. It was obvious that the employees knew the owner and the owner knew his employees - he cared about his sheep.

Investing in the Future

In *The Seven Habits of Highly Effective People,* author Stephen Covey talks about making deposits into an emotional bank account.[4] I saw this leader demonstrating this principle throughout the day of the strategic planning seminar. The owner had an *investment* in his employees beyond monetary parameters. He was also open to his fellow workers in a personal, vulnerable way, allowing them to know him as a caring human being. The *deposits* he made that day, and that he continues to make in his routine business practices, are relationship reserves from which he can make withdrawals in tough times.

An Egalitarian Ideal

Sergeant Mike Strank was one of the men who raised the American flag at Iwo Jima. He wasn't a corporate executive or a business owner. He probably didn't know anything about strategic plans, missions, or leadership models. But he was what his men called a "Marine's Marine," the best leader they ever had. This must have been true because they followed him into that firestorm at Iwo Jima. Here's how one of them described Mike shortly before they landed:

> Mike is their shepherd. He has won their confidence . . . Mike, the immigrant American, is representative of the best of the young leaders in the Pacific. A sergeant, he does not lord his rank over anyone. He embodies the Raider egalitarian ideal of no divisions between the men, no

hierarchy.

He eats with his men instead of going to the sergeants' mess. And a few weeks before leaving for Iwo Jima, Captain Dave Severance tries to recommend Mike for the rank of Platoon Sergeant. Mike turns the offer down on the spot, saying, "I promised my boys I'd be there for them."[5]

Mike was the embodiment of the SE leader. He led his men; he didn't drive them. He knew and cared about them, ultimately giving his life with and for those he led. Those he led followed him into battle—many of them to their own deaths—because they trusted him. That's what SE leadership is all about.

Summary: Know Thyself

As you have seen in this brief overview of leadership theories, there are admirable qualities in each of the leadership theories. However, it is a huge mistake to exercise the principles of one theory alone—especially those who are seeking to become effective leaders. Sticking with one leadership theory leaves an important component out of the equation—those being led.

The truth is that effective leaders find themselves using aspects of all the theories at some time during the challenging business of leading. It is important, however, to do a careful self-analysis to determine your dominant leadership methodology. You must know how you *tend* to lead before you can ever do anything to improve your leadership style.

You must also have an understanding of how those you are

trying to lead need to be led. For example, let's say you are a Theory SE leader. You believe in your employees and want them to succeed so that the organization can succeed. However, one of your employees consistently arrives late for work and doesn't fulfill the requirements of the job you have given him. Because of this, he is adversely affecting the morale of the other employees and the business as a whole. You care about him, but feel he is taking advantage of you. What do you do? Quite simply, if you really care for the employee, you may have to Theory X him for a while in order to best serve his long-term interests.

My experience has been that the most effective leaders are those who understand various theories, applying the appropriate principles at the appropriate times—ensuring the success of the company and the employees. Effective leaders are those who have a palette full of leadership knowledge.

Self-Assessment Exercise:

1. Write down which leadership theory you believe is your normal style. List five specific examples to demonstrate how you operate from this theory.

2. When you are being led, what circumstances make you feel most productive and fulfilled?

3. When you are being led, what circumstances make you feel most negative about your tasks?

4. How do you think others would view your ability to lead?

5. Do you need to alter your leadership style? If so, why? How do you propose changing? If you do not feel the need to alter your leadership style, why do you believe you are successful in your present style?

Finally: Share the results of your self-assessment with someone you know will be truthful with you. Have him or her assess your answers and see if you have an accurate picture of your leadership characteristics. Many times, how we perceive ourselves and how those we are leading perceive us are two very different things. It is important to know ourselves and those we lead.

Case Scenario

A new leader is hired at a company. Even though the earnings have been increasing under the old leadership, they have not increased at the level the Board of Directors and the stockholders desire. The former leader was popular, charismatic and had grown the company each year under his leadership.

The interview and selection process has had negative effects on the company culture and morale is very low because the company has been without effective leadership during the transition process.

At the first gathering of the leader's leadership team (none of whom had been involved in the selection process) the new leader announces his decision to make severe cutbacks in staff and management as well.

As questions arise during the meeting, the leader informs the team that they will be given information on an "as needed" basis only and that he will meet with them on an individual basis to discuss their status and the status of those in their respective departments.

1. What kind of a leader do you believe this person to be?

2. What effect will this first meeting have on corporate culture and morale?

3. What would be your suggestions about on how you would have handled this meeting if, in fact, the actions the new leader described are actually needed?

4. Describe (or rewrite) the actions in this situation from a Theory SE perspective.

1 For example, see Paul Hersey and Kenneth H. Blanchard, *Manage
   ment of Organizational Behavior: Utilizing Human Resources,* 4th
   ed. (Ontario: Prentice-Hall, 1982).

2 For more information on McGregor's theories, see Douglas
   McGregor, *The Human Side of Enterprise* (New York: McGraw-
   Hill, 1960) and *Leadership and Motivation* (MA: MIT Press,
   1966).

3 For more information, see William G. Ouchi, *Theory Z* (Avon, NY:
   Avon Books, 1982).

4 Stephen Covey, *The 7 Habits of Highly Effective People: Powerful Les
   sons in Personal Change* (New York: A Fireside Book, 1990).

5 James Bradley and Ron Powers, *Flags of Our Fathers* (New
   York: Bantam Books, 2000), 132.

CHAPTER

2

SOLID SUPPORT
The Leadership Tripod Legs

The Leadership Tripod Legs

In our *Leadership Tripod* model, leadership stands on the tripod. The top piece would be meaningless without something upon which to stand. The tripod provides that support, making true, effective leadership possible.

A few years ago when I first began to construct this model of leadership, I first came up with the idea of a triangle. The three pivotal elements—responsibility, authority, and accountability—certainly fit that triangle model. Each is dependent on the other. If one is absent, the model is flawed. Thus, leadership cannot and will not be effective.

However, the triangle is one dimensional, however. I was looking for a model with more depth, one that would convey the idea of structural support. The tripod was the perfect solution. The image of three legs supporting the primary concept captured the essence of what I was trying to depict—providing a stable base upon which leadership could anchor itself. If a leg were missing, the tripod could not stand. If a leg were weak, the tripod could collapse. If the legs were not of equal length, the top piece would be in danger of falling. The tripod then becomes a good metaphor for leadership. A leader could have all the skills, traits, and behaviors necessary for success, but without the three supporting legs of responsibility, authority, and accountability, he or she would not be able to effectively lead an organization.

Ask yourself these questions:
1. Can a leader lead effectively if he or she is given *responsibility* and held *accountable*, but is not given the *authority* to make decisions?
2. Can a leader lead effectively if he or she is given *responsi-*

bility and *authority*, but then is not held *accountable?*

3.   Can a leader lead effectively if he or she is given *authority* and held *accountable*, but is given no *responsibility?*

In my opinion and as the result of years of both leading and observing leaders, I believe the answer to be an emphatic *NO* to all of the questions above. Each of the three legs is equally important in assuring that leadership is securely held in place. If they are not structurally sound and firmly planted, effective leadership will be compromised—and the organization and those being led will not reach their full potential for excellence.

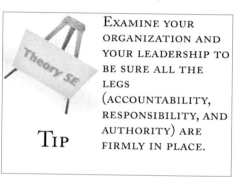

EXAMINE YOUR ORGANIZATION AND YOUR LEADERSHIP TO BE SURE ALL THE LEGS (ACCOUNTABILITY, RESPONSIBILITY, AND AUTHORITY) ARE FIRMLY IN PLACE.

TIP

As we take a look at each of these three legs, I ask you to relate what you learn in the next few pages to your own organizations and to your own experience as a leader or potential leader. I think you will find, as I have, that this tripod model is applicable to any situation.

Responsibility

The word *responsibility* probably means many things to many people. Therein lies the fundamental reason why the responsibilities of a leader need to be as clearly defined as possible. Those in leadership positions realize all too well how difficult it is to put down on paper the responsibilities entailed in their everyday schedules. It isn't as simple as just listing them and then checking them off as you accomplish them each day. Some things seem to defy description. For example, a leader is expected to facilitate intra- and interdepartmental communication, develop networking with other organizations, establish rapport with personnel and clients, and a host of other hard-to-define responsibilities. Leadership responsibilities are not exactly the same as checking items off your weekend chore list, are they?

The Importance of a Job Description

When it comes to itemizing job responsibilities, most of us immediately think of that familiar term: the *job description*. Familiar or not, it is amazing to me how many large companies, school corporations, small businesses, and churches lack even the most basic job description for *any* level of responsibility—leader or those under leadership. Most often, the tasks are simply done and no one knows specifically what is entailed in positions outside one's own sphere of responsibility, nor how these various areas relate to one another. While an organization can function this way for a while, problems arise when a gap occurs: someone leaves, is injured or falls ill, or even dies.

Organizations with no clear-cut job descriptions then scramble to fill the void. Many times tasks are not completed, clients are left hanging, and money is lost because no one initially took the time to list the specific responsibilities for the position in which the void occurred.

Avoid a Power Play

A dangerous situation can sometimes occur in organizations that allow people to develop the responsibilities of their own positions—without requiring them to document these responsibilities. Such people can cling tightly to their positions without ever allowing anyone else to know the specifics of their jobs. This is called wielding "expert power," a kind of power play most frequently seen in long-time employees who want to insure job security. "If no one else knows what exactly it is that I do," such a person reasons, "no one else can take my job." For obvious reasons, a leader cannot allow this to happen in any organization he or she is charged to lead. I have personally seen this kind of power play cripple organizations, essentially rendering them helpless because of an unexpected void in a key position. For example, what would happen if the only person who knew the passwords to the accounting software package died overnight of a heart attack? How would payroll be accomplished, bills paid and collections made?

All Dressed Up and No Place to Go!

The opposite can also occur if detailed responsibilities are not given to leaders and those they are supposed to lead. A leader or an employee cannot be expected to perform effectively if none of them have a job description.

As hard as it is to believe, this does happen all too frequently today. It even happened to me. Not long after I retired, I was asked by an organization to take a leadership position. A friend in this organization asked me to serve. I told the friend that I would lead this organization on an interim basis until he found someone permanent. After all, I was looking forward to retirement!

So I rearranged my life to fit the time requirements of the position, and decided to tackle the task with enthusiasm. Much to my surprise and dismay, I found I had no specific responsibility. Essentially, I had been placed, but found myself doing little for the organization. Because the associated responsibilities of the position were not given to me specifically, others began to assume the leader's responsibilities. They assumed these responsibilities because they felt by doing so, their own positions would be strengthened.

This is not a good situation for any organization and can be very demoralizing for a new leader. When a new leader is selected for a position in which responsibility has been shifted to others, or others have taken the responsibility upon themselves, it may be difficult for the new leader to recapture the responsibility he or she needs to be an effective leader. Anyone confronting such a situation needs to immediately "reclaim territory" or he/she will be ineffective.

Off Center

Without the solid leg of *Responsibility*, the Leadership Tripod cannot stand. It will be off-center and in danger of crashing to the ground—taking with it the hopes and unrealized potential of those affected in any way by leadership.

What is the answer to this unbalanced distribution of responsibility? For maximum efficiency and overall stability, specific job descriptions are needed at every level. If employees are going to be given authority and held accountable for the functions of their positions, it only makes sense for them to know the specifics of their responsibilities.

From Custodian to CEO

In creating job descriptions for an organization, from custodian to CEO, no position is exempt. While some employees
may "look down" on the custodial aspects of their organization—pointing to the lower pay scale and perceived lower status
of custodians—I know for a fact how instrumental this position
is to the smooth operation of any organization.

My father was a school custodian. Let's compare the everyday responsibilities of a school custodian as they relate to the
education of the children with the everyday responsibilities
of a school board member or even the superintendent. If the
school board member and the custodian were each to fail in
their respective responsibilities for one day, which do you think
would most impact the students? Which abdication of duty
would most negatively affect the learning environment, prevent-
ing students from learning and teachers from teaching? Which
one—the custodian or the school board member—could be
absent for a day and probably not even be missed? When one
realizes the more immediate impact of the custodian on the day
to day functioning of the school, rather than the less immediate impact of the school board member, it makes one pause for
thought, doesn't it?

The job description for a school custodian is certainly more
than a one-page "clean your area" kind of summary. Being a
custodian involves everything from coordinating the cleaning and maintaining of facilities, to the types of chemicals to
be used and their proper application, to the correct storage of
those chemicals and disposal of waste, to the proper care and
maintenance of equipment. The custodian must perform all of
these responsibilities while adhering to the school's mission:

assuring each student a quality educational experience because of the custodian's part in preparing, maintaining, and cleaning the rooms in which that education will take place. While not diminishing the importance of a governing board, hopefully, you can see that on a daily basis, the custodian's responsibilities are paramount to the mission of educating children.

This kind of specific job description needs to be written for members at every level of the organization. What this job description can further do is to give each position a sense of how they "fit" into the organization and how their role assists the company in reaching its vision and mission.

Securing the Strong Leg

All areas of responsibility in an organization should have job descriptions with that kind of detail, laying out specific tasks and timeline expectations. Many firms will make a cursory attempt at providing job descriptions for the more high-profile positions, but seem hesitant to take the time to profile job descriptions for every position in an organization. One very efficient way to accomplish this seemingly daunting task is to ask the employees themselves to help in the creation of the job descriptions. Writing their own job descriptions will give employees a part in implementing organizational policy, while at the same time demonstrating how the company values them and their place in the organization. The initial work of creating job descriptions will be well worth the effort, resulting in more competent cross training and promotions, as well as aiding in more timely and efficient replacement decisions.

To be as effective as possible and to continue to improve their competitive edge, organizations must develop *Responsibil-*

ity, placing its strong leg securely under their leadership team and other stakeholders as well.

Authority

Webster's Dictionary defines authority as (n) *"the right and power to command and be obeyed or to do something."*

I think we capture more of the grit of this word when we look at the verb form of the definition: (v) *"to give legal power or right to."*

In leadership, the power and right to make decisions is the authority a leader needs to carry out leadership effectively. A leader can be given much responsibility, but if not then given the authority to fulfill the responsibility, his or her leadership will be undermined.

Running on Empty

Let's compare a leader to the owner of a fine car. The car owner has been equipped with an adequate means of transportation and even may have been given a road map to guide him to his destination. But someone forgot to put gas in the tank of the car. After traveling a short distance, the gas tank runs dry and the driver is forced to pull the car over to the side of the road. Given responsibility (and maybe even a detailed job description) but no fuel (authority), the driver is left behind, unable to move forward or merge with traffic, unable to travel down the road of self-improvement and company success.

Why does this happen? Why would any organization give a leader or prospective leader responsibility, but not the authority to fulfill the obligations (and potential) of that responsibility? I have come to the conclusion that some of those who hire and place leaders are either frustrated individuals who would like to be leaders themselves, or are power hungry and insecure, exercising control over a situation by "controlling" the leader.

This failure to equip leaders with the authority to fulfill their responsibilities is counterproductive in every way, but it is a phenomenon It happens in every type of organization from churches to large corporations. Many times it occurs when a leader leaves the organization to go to a different position. You can almost hear the vacuum of authority being sucked out from the position and being taken over by Boards.

Foul Ball!

We are all familiar with professional sports franchise owners famous for "dis-empowering" their managers. Although they select and hire their leaders—which is their prerogative as principal owners—they all too often undercut their leaders' ability to do the job they were hired to do. News stories abound of continuing intrusions, overstepping the authority of the managers and coaches, making decisions the manager should make, and keeping the team in constant turmoil. As a result, some club owners have gone through an embarrassingly long list of managers, coaches and general managers over the years. This is a classic example of how to effectively sabotage responsibility: shut it down by refusing to activate it with the corresponding catalyst of authority.

In *The 21 Irrefutable Laws of Leadership,* John Maxwell states, "Only secure leaders are able to give power to others."[1] I believe this maxim to be true not only of leaders, but of those who select leaders. If a board, owner, supervisor, team leader, or any other person or group cannot release power to the leaders under them, allowing these leaders to make and implement decisions, the organization, company, leadership group, team, or even family will fall short of its full potential. In fact, withholding authority can lead to disaster.

Learning the Hard Way

President John F. Kennedy is one of our most admired and beloved presidents. But even he had to learn a lesson about leadership the hard way. In making the decision to invade the Bay of Pigs, he failed to relinquish authority to the appropriate leaders. History tells us that he held tight reins on those in authority, made the major decisions himself, and listened to few people outside the close-knit inner circle of his Cabinet. In doing this, a kind of "Group Think" took place. Many advisers who should have been involved in such an important determination were left out of the decision-making loop. Even though their offices and roles carried appropriate responsibility, they were given no authority to make suggestions or decisions. If President Kennedy had allowed them to exercise their authority, the decision most likely would have been not to invade. But our country did invade, with disastrous results.

However, in a later situation, President Kennedy did make the most of his leaders and advisers, allowing them to exercise their authority while he seriously weighed their recommendations. He also included proven leaders outside the Washington circuit, empowering them to speak their minds and allowing them to make decisions. In so doing, he defused the volatile Cuban Missile Crisis—one of his greatest achievements and finest hours. President Kennedy learned from his mistakes how to relinquish power and trust his leaders to do their jobs—not necessarily giving him what he wanted, but what they thought to be the best possible solution to the problem. Two critical situations were handled in two totally different ways with dramatically different results.

I am told that Theodore Roosevelt once said, "The best executive is the one who has sense enough to pick good men to do what he wants done, and self-restraint enough to keep from meddling with them while they do it."

This statement sums up what leadership authority should be. Those who refuse to share authority believe they are making themselves and their organizations stronger. In fact, the opposite is most times true.

Hoarding Authority

The devastating effect of hoarding authority is well illustrated in the failure of many small businesses to make it to "the next level." In this scenario, an entrepreneur starts a business and is the primary force behind its growth and success. Then the business arrives at the point where it outgrows the entrepreneur's ability to lead it by him or herself. The leader faces an important decision. Does the owner hire managers and give them the responsibility and authority to expand the growth potential, or does he or she continue to "run the show" all alone? Unfortunately, if the owner hoards authority and responsibility, he or she will experience one or more of the following: 1) the owner/entrepreneur will burn out, 2) the company will remain at status quo, or 3) the company will begin the slow slide to failure. If the original founder of the company does not carefully select and mentor a successor, there is a high probability that the company will not continue to exist after the original founder is out of the picture. Hoarding authority will most assuredly choke the life out of the very dream he or she had for the company's success.

On the Other Hand

Just as denying authority to those in leadership positions can debilitate an organization's forward movement, so too can granting too much authority. Granting authority without sufficient checks and balances (accountability) can be destructive to effective leadership and can sabotage the entire organization. As we saw earlier in our discussion of responsibility, a leader or one under leadership who is given absolute authority without the corresponding balance of accountability is in danger of wielding expert power.

In other words, expert power exists when someone in the organization has knowledge that no one else in the organization has. If that person is terminated, leaves voluntarily, or becomes incapacitated, the organization can suffer a crushing blow because of the void that person leaves.

I know of a small corporation with a technology leader who had expert power. He was the only one in the organization with the passwords to enable the computer system. When he suddenly became critically ill, the corporation was literally incapacitated because no one couldn't access their computers. Valuable time and resources were lost until they located an outside "expert" to override the system.

The technology leader of this organization had been given responsibility and authority. However, no one had held him accountable for seeing that an emergency plan was in place to prevent just such an organizational collapse. With that in mind, let's turn to the third leg of the leadership tripod—the leg of accountability.

Accountability

Not long ago on my way to the university, I was reminded of what *accountability* means in a very personal (and expensive) way. Driving with my sunroof open, I was really enjoying the cool rush of air around me, the early morning sunshine, and the smell of newly mowed grass. You know how a car just seems to run smoother after it has been washed and waxed? Well, if you do, you can picture the joy I was experiencing as my freshly cleaned car cut swiftly through the cool morning air on my drive through beautiful central Indiana. Swiftly is the operative word here. I was having such a good time, I failed to realize I was speeding. Just as I thought things couldn't get any better than this, I spotted a distinctive car in the opposite lane—a big black car with many antennas and the markings of the Indiana State Police. Instinctively, I checked my speedometer and realized I was going at least ten to twelve miles per hour over the posted speed limit. Glancing guiltily in my rearview mirror, I saw the police officer nimbly turn around and head in my direction. No doubt about it: I was about to be held *accountable* for my decision to drive over the speed limit. This lesson in accountability cost me $99.50! While that amount would make most of us say, "Ouch!", just think how much more expensive the cost was for the company that didn't hold its technology expert accountable for his actions?

Is Accountability a Negative?

In successful leadership, accountability is not an option—it is a necessity. This third leg of the tripod is essential for effective leadership. Without accountability, the organization will never be what it should or could be.

Why is accountability necessary? We have only to look at our government's fundamental structure to see the reason why. Our founding fathers created the executive, legislative, and judicial branches of government as a check-and-balance system; i.e., to keep one leg of government from overpowering or disempowering another.

The *Leadership Tripod* works in the same way. Accountability is necessary as a check and balance to assure that all tasks are completed, to assess the organization's movement toward continuous improvement, and to determine if employee and organizational needs are being met. If performed properly, accountability will help all the personnel as well as the organization reach their highest potential.

Over the years, the main problem I have seen in the judicious use of accountability is in how it is *perceived*. Many in leadership see accountability in a very negative light. They see it as punitive, rather than as a tool meant to foster their growth and effectiveness, as well as that of the company or organization. In this "negative" light, accountability has been viewed primarily as a performance evaluation, telling people what they are doing wrong. In a more "positive" light, however, accountability can be used to affirm their worth and motivation to improve.

"Likert" or Not

Many companies and most organizations employ a standard procedure to *evaluate* staff. This term even suggests a "summative" process of sorts to determine if a person stays or goes. The Likert Scale is one such evaluation method, listing categories on a scale of one to five—one representing "strongly disagree" and five representing "strongly agree." Sometimes the scale is reversed and sometimes more than five numbers are used. A person's value is measured in those narrowly defined and impersonal categories. This evaluation may attempt to broach the areas of goal setting or self-improvement, but generally this process is highly subjective and evaluator-driven, with little if any input from the one being evaluated.

Future-oriented leaders must replace the negative "keep-or-lose-your-job" focus of the evaluation form and develop a positive paradigm of improvement through accountability. When looking at many of these evaluation processes, I have found it possible for a form to be honestly completed and yet not actually reflect the true performance of the employee being evaluated. This type of evaluation can miss on both sides of the spectrum. It can make an employee's performance look much better or much worse than it actually is. The standard forms and processes are many times just too simplistic.

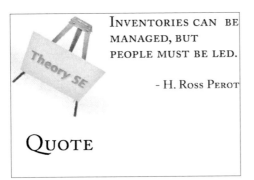

INVENTORIES CAN BE MANAGED, BUT PEOPLE MUST BE LED.

- H. Ross Perot

QUOTE

Formative, Not Just Summative

We should probably even go so far as to change our nomenclature for this entire process. Rather than talking about "evaluation," we should probably be talking about assessment. To do true assessment, we need to examine different types of accountability.

For assessment to be effective for all those involved in an organization, my belief is that accountability must be "formative" as well as "summative." What I mean by formative is that accountability should not just be judgmental, based on what the person has or has not done, but accountability should also be a mutual attempt to identify and describe what the person needs to do to improve, including what specific things can make him or her a better employee or leader. By making this a mutual effort, employees are not only held accountable for what their supervisors say they must do, but they learn valuable, transferable skills designed to improve their performance. This kind of accountability gives them "buy-in" on improvement at all levels. This improvement process should also be tied in to the overall improvement (strategic plan) of the organization. In this way, the person understands and internalizes how through his or her individual improvement, the organization can move toward the corporate goals it has set for all concerned. I also believe that as often as possible, these goal setting activities should be led by the person being held accountable. If the evaluee can help develop and implement plans for their own improvement, there will be less question about ownership of these goals.

I have been working with two different organizations to totally redesign their methods of accountability. Accountability in these organizations has traditionally not been questioned.

The traditional flow looks like this:

Job description——-Some sort of documentation——-Evaluation

What we are trying to create now is far different and will take time to fully implement into the organizational culture:

Job description——-----Assessment————-Verification

Instead of using Likert Scales, we are developing rubrics to assess the achievement of success and the level of success attained. This will take most of the subjectivity from the assessment process, thus reducing the level of apprehension in both the assessor and the one being assessed.

The huge difference between the two methods is that the person to be assessed or held accountable will know *beforehand* how he or she will be assessed and what specifically he or she will need to achieve. The one assessing, as well as the one who will be assessed will know up front what both are looking for and what has to take place for successful achievement of the goals.

This process will be viewed not as a method of *separating out the poor performers*, but of *improving an individual's job performance*. The leader will not be perceived as trying to "catch the person doing something wrong" (Theory X, SW), but rather the evaluator will be looking at how both leader and employee can work together to improve themselves and the organization as a whole (Theory Y, Z, SE).

Exceptions

Just as we saw earlier in the section on responsibility, there will still be instances when a very specific, documented "do-it-or-you-won't-stay-here" type of evaluation will be necessary. There are always those who simply won't do what they are supposed to do, no matter how you try to motivate them. In some cases, accountability necessitates removing poor perform-ers from their jobs for the good of the other employees and the organization as a whole. It is never pleasant to have to terminate employees, especially in the traditional evaluation process. But the damaging effects can be minimized by changing the assess-ment process to one based on formative values. With a formative assessment process, those involved will have been made aware of potential problems well in advance of dismissal, and will have been given ample opportunities to make needed improvements.

If done properly, staff will not have to be terminated as often by the leader; they will terminate themselves. When everyone knows exactly what is expected, the leader and the staff person will completely understand the consequences when expectations are not met.

Summary: Driving Home a Point

All three legs of the leadership tripod—*Responsibility, Authority,* and *Accountability*—must be present for effective leadership to occur. Those under leadership must also be able to identify and understand these principles. To "drive home" my point, let's look at my experience with the state trooper as it relates to this model.

The State Trooper

When the state trooper stopped me to give me a ticket, it was evident that he knew his *Responsibility*. He understood his job description because it was very specifically laid out for him in the code of law by which our state operates. He knew what he was supposed to do. He knew on that lovely spring morning that his specific assignment was to cover State Highway 37 in Madison County. He also knew he had the *Authority* to stop a certain motorist for going too fast and to issue him a ticket. He knew further that if he didn't do his job correctly, he would have to face *Accountability* in a court of law. Therefore, he filled out the ticket correctly and made sure the motorist knew why the trooper was issuing the ticket.

What would have happened, instead, if the trooper:

- had responsibility and was held accountable, but had no authority to issue the ticket?
- had authority and was held accountable, but was given no responsibility?
- had responsibility and authority, but was not held accountable?

I believe you can use your imagination to envision the chaos that could take place.

The Driver

What about the driver? He had *Responsibility* because he had read the driver's manual, knew the laws, and knew the posted speed limit. He had *Authority* because he could make the decision on how fast to drive, where to drive, what to drive, etc. He also certainly was held *Accountable* for his actions when the officer pulled him over and issued him a ticket.

What would have happened, instead, if . . .

You can take yourself through the same exercise above and get the picture. The ramifications of a driver not being held accountable for speeding could result in the ultimate price: the loss of his life or the life of someone else.

Self-Assessment Exercise

1. In your leadership position, are your responsibilities clearly defined?
    a. If yes, how?
    b. If no, why not, and what can you do to change this?

2. Do you as a leader make clear the responsibilities of those you lead:
    a. If yes, how?
    b. If no, why not, and what can you do to correct this?

3. In your leadership position, do you have the authority needed to do your job effectively?
    a. If yes, how?
    b. If no, why not, and what can you do to change this?

4. Do you as a leader give those you lead the authority they need to do their jobs effectively?
    a. If yes, how?
    b. If no, why not, and what should you do to correct this?

5. In your leadership position, are you held accountable for your actions and performance?
    a. If yes, how?
    b. If no, why not, and what can you do to change this?

6. Are those you lead accountable for their performance and improvement?
    a. If yes, how?
    b. If no, why not, and how can you change this?

Case Scenario

You have been given information that company X is searching for a new leader. A peer has suggested that the position might be one you would be or should be interested in seeking.

Your present position has been rewarding and you feel comfortable in your present role, but lately you feel you may have outgrown the company's ability to challenge you and your abilities. Since you always want to be productive and continue to improve yourself, you decide to pursue the opportunity.

You inquire about the opening and send a resume. You are contacted by the new employer and an interview is scheduled. Based on what you've read and learned thus far...

1. How will you plan for the interview?

2. What specific questions will you be prepared to answer?

3. What specific questions will you be prepared to ask?

4. How will you handle the situation with your present employer?

1   John Maxwell, *The 21 Irrefutable Laws of Leadership* (Nashville:
       Thomas Nelson, 1998), 124.

Theory SE

CHAPTER 3

BRACED ON FOCUS
STRATEGIC PLANNING

Strategic Planning

Introduction: The Tripod Braces

I would like the reader to visualize the Leadership Tripod and imagine a huge boulder suddenly dropped onto the top piece or platform of the tripod. Supporting this enormous weight are the three solid legs of Responsibility, Authority, and Accountability. Although they manage to hold up under this burden for a while, eventually the unrelenting weight of the boulder is going to take its toll. The stress on the legs will be too much and they will weaken, tilt, or collapse under the pressure. One does not have to think long about what kinds of events that could make the *Leadership Tripod* collapse: economic changes; political changes; or loss of key personnel to cite a few.

The legs of the *Tripod* by themselves are not enough to ensure structural viability. Braces would strengthen the tripod, giving additional support to the legs and helping to distribute the weight.

This, of course, is a perfect analogy for our study of leadership. What components are necessary to strengthen and stabilize a company through its leadership?

In my years of consulting with a variety of companies and organizations, I have identified three characteristics or "constants" essential to bracing the leadership tripod, pulling it together and making it strong:

1. An effective strategic planning process and plan implementation.
2. Effective and ongoing analysis of communications.
3. Values and beliefs upon which a company builds strong ethics and morals.

In this and the next two chapters, I will discuss these three characteristics in detail and give specific ways to implement them. Those in leadership positions can sometimes be overwhelmed by the enormity of their tasks and the sheer number of people for whom they are responsible. Like the boulder sitting on the tripod platform, without a solid framework to bear the burden of leadership, the whole structure is in danger of collapse or at least not being as strong as it could and should be.

Fate or Focus?

We hear a lot about strategic planning these days. It's one of our most popular "buzz" phrases. So why is it significant, and why have I chosen *strategic planning* as one of the braces holding the *Leadership Tripod* together?

In my own eight-year experience with a company moving from a Theory X to a Theory Y frame of reference, I have found strategic planning to be indispensable in developing the company's course and fostering overall improvement. I have also read and studied extensively about how to change the leadership style of an organization, and consulted with flourishing companies as I "picked the brains" of successful leaders. All of this has reinforced my belief that strategic planning is instrumental in making leadership effective and in moving a company toward continuous improvement (see Appendix I).

Strategic plans are not just for big corporations and organizations. Individuals and families can benefit greatly from strategic planning. About ten years ago, I created a strategic plan for my own life. It has been one of the most significant events in my life and in the life of my family. The process caused me to look more deeply into how I was living, compelling me to prioritize my actions and create a self-improvement plan.

A company without a strategic plan is like a ship without a rudder. It most certainly can move across the water, but no one knows where it will end up. Likewise, an individual or family without a plan embarks on a journey through life with no road map. Where they end up is wherever fate takes them, and that most likely is not where they can live most fully and productively.

Over the past several years, I have taught strategic planning principles and have had the opportunity to facilitate the strategic planning process in many areas and situations across the country. The different types and sizes of the companies do dictate somewhat the time necessary to develop an effective plan, but the process works in companies of any size or setting—just as it will work well with individuals and families. The process I have developed is succinct and can be completed in as little as two days and for very little outlay of capital and resources. It does result, however, in a complete document that can be used as a roadmap for improvement. It is a simple, but useful way to plan for the continuous improvement all organizations need.

Thinking Strategically

TIP

YOUR VISION MUST BE FIRMLY IN PLACE SO THAT ALL STAKEHOLDERS KNOW WHERE THE ORGANIZATION IS GOING IN THE NEAR AND DISTANT FUTURE. IF YOU DON'T KNOW WHERE YOU ARE GOING, HOW WILL YOU KNOW WHEN YOU GET THERE?

My first question to a group trying to learn about strategic planning is this: "If you don't know where you are going, how do you know when you get there?"

The simplicity of this question underscores a truth few individuals and companies take seriously. Many families, companies, churches, and other organizations operate in a totally *reactive* mode, almost never exercising control over their destiny by taking the time to plan strategically.

My family and I recently made an emergency trip to Cincinnati to be with my brother who had just suffered a heart attack. When we were given the message that my brother was ill, did we just jump in the car and take off? No, we called and got the name of the hospital, then searched the Internet for specific directions on how to get there.

Had we just jumped in the car and sped away, we might somehow have found the hospital, but it would not have been without great loss of time, many frustrations, and possible dangers. By taking the time to plan strategically and set out our goals, we were able to make efficient use of our time and we arrived at the hospital safely, serving our family's needs in a most effective manner.

Why should we do anything less for our families or for the organizations we serve? Making decisions like: a) launching a new product; b) making drastic staff cuts; or c) acquiring a competitor without proper planning can be like jumping in a car without a detailed map.

Streamlining the Process

Another observation I have made over the past few years is the time and effort many companies waste trying to develop a strategic plan. While recognizing the need for a strategic plan, they have been thwarted in their efforts because they have been sold a process that is cumbersome and time consuming. I know of one corporation that spent thousands of dollars and eighteen months in developing a plan that still has not been completed. The stakeholders became frustrated with the whole ordeal. For eighteen months everyone had been talking about change and direction, but nothing had happened. If you can't develop a plan in a much shorter time frame than eighteen months, then you are probably not using a method conducive to productive planning strategies. The reality is that if the strategic planning takes eighteen months to complete, the original emphasis could easily be outdated by the time the plan is finalized.

The simple process I have developed has been field tested and proven to be effective. Of course, the process it continues to be improved—that's the point of strategic planning, after all. Many of the earlier idiosyncrasies were a natural outcome of trial and error, but all were useful in helping to sharpen and streamline the process and make it more user friendly.

Simplistically the organization develops a vision, mission, goals and objectives. As you will see, the vision and mission are never referred to as "statements". This may seem a small thing, but it isn't. When companies and organizations refer to vision and mission "statements" the words vision and mission become adjectives and the word statement becomes the noun. This sends a wrong message to all concerned. The vision and mission should be the noun, not the statement. The focus needs to be on the vision and mission. They need to be viable, real and able for all stakeholders to accept and internalize.

Establishing Parameters

Some preparatory work is necessary before launching into the work of building a strategic plan. The company or organization will need to decide who is going to be involved in the planning group, how often to meet before and after the plan is established, who will be responsible for "activating" the plan, and how to assure that everyone is on the same page when it comes to interpreting the purpose of the plan.

Get Them Involved!

The makeup of the planning group is critical. What I have found over the years is that the more stakeholders are included in the process, the more effective the planning and strategic plan will be. Initially, until the decision-makers understand the process, they may need to create a rudimentary plan or prototype for the overall company. As soon as possible, however, as many levels of stakeholders as possible should be included in the process and allowed to modify and fine-tune the prototype. This will give them a sense of ownership in formulating the plan, rather than feeling that those "in charge" imposed it on them. Top down plans may look good on paper, but will likely not be readily accepted by stakeholders who have no representation on the planning team.

Visit It Often

The planning process isn't over when the strategic plan is created. A strategic plan isn't a document that is filed away and forgotten. Strategic planning is ongoing. At the very least, the planning process should take place annually. Some companies in fast-changing, competitive environments may have to plan on a more frequent basis. Once the plan has been completed, it should be revisited on no less than a quarterly basis. If possible, organizations and companies should revisit it even more frequently. In this way, the company expresses to its constituents the importance and viability of the strategic plan.

A strategic plan that has been developed and then forgotten is worse than no plan at all. If stakeholders have been through the process and have the expectations the plan will be implemented and then no action occurs, they will become disillusioned with the plan, the process, and the leadership who has proposed the initiative. In the several years I have been fortunate to have led organizations through this process the leadership failed to follow through only a few times. I am convinced in those cases it would have been better to have done nothing rather than creating a good plan, then leaving it in a drawer.

Activate It

The plan also needs to include details on its activation. How will it be implemented, and who in the organization will be responsible for making sure each phase is completed? Some leaders mistakenly believe that once the plan has been completed, their responsibility is to oversee and complete all the items contained in the plan. Rather than make the leader stronger, this just adds more weight to the "boulder of responsibility" pressing down on the leader, a condition that will only weaken that person.

In *Leadership by the Book,* the authors write, "Leaders often just don't know how to develop people, and they end up doing all the work themselves. In addition to burning themselves out, their people remain dependent on them and underdeveloped."[1] This is what could and sometimes does happen if leaders don't share the responsibility of putting the strategic plan into action.

Author Dr. Eugene White in his book, *Leadership Beyond Excuses*, uses the metaphor of a leader on the end of a rope to emphasize how important it is to empower the stakeholders in the organization to implement the plan. Dr. White begins his metaphor with the description of a group of followers hanging by a rope over a cliff. By the end of the metaphor, the leader as well as those being led, are sharing the responsibility of holding the rope and walking on the same path towards excellence. That path is the strategic plan in action. The strategic plan is not the leader's responsibility alone, nor is it the leader's plan alone. It belongs to the entire organization. When all pull together, great things can happen to an organization and its stakeholders.[2]

Understand It

PLANNING IS BRINGING THE FUTURE INTO THE PRESENT SO THAT YOU CAN DO SOME-THING ABOUT IT NOW.

QUOTE

- ALAN LAKEIN

Some leaders don't understand that the strategic plan is a guide, not a barrier, to continuous improvement and change. As I mentioned earlier, the process I will be discussing has been modified through trial and error. One corporation I led through the process seemed to flourish. It appeared the plan was being implemented very effectively. I called the leader to see how things were progressing. He said enthusiastically, "Great! Every time someone comes in to ask to do something, I just pull out the plan. And I say, 'So, if it's not on the plan, we won't be doing it.'"

Obviously, this leader had to be mentored further! He had to learn that the goal of a strategic plan is not to limit what a company can do; it should just set the minimum level of progress for improvement. Now each time I lead an organization through this process for the first time, I try to impress upon them that planning is a minimum standard of success, not a maximum. The plan should be a springboard to improvement not a finish line for completion.

The Strategic Plan: A Model

If the reader can imagine a body of water with no banks, you can imagine a company, family or organization without a strategic plan. There may be many good things in the water, but without boundaries and direction, the water becomes essentially a swamp. We equate swamps with stagnation; very little of anything positive comes from them and the water goes nowhere.

If, however, you put banks around that same water and give the water direction, it begins to move. Flowing water is active and productive. It can generate electricity, provide nourishment to wildlife, become a habitat for fish and other animals, provide people opportunities for recreation to people, etc. So it is with companies, families, and organizations. They can be much more productive if given the direction of a strategic plan.

Appendix I of this book contains an example of a corporate strategic plan, as well as a personal strategic plan. These plans are from a *real* company and a *real* person. After you have read the specific sections of the Strategic Planning Model below, go to the appendix and read the corresponding elements in the real-life examples.

The Strategic Planning Model below flows in a circular direction. As those who have studied or completed a strategic plan realize, a circle never ends. To be effective, a strategic planning process must be ongoing—constantly being updated to assure that the individual or organization is on track for continuous improvement. The following model is understandable and easy to apply:

Strategic Planning Model

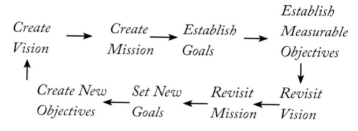

This model builds on itself. As you will read later, each section goes together like a puzzle and if one is not accomplished the picture of success will not be complete.

Let's examine the individual components of the model to see how you or your organization can readily adapt this model to your particular circumstances.

Vision: How Do You Want to Be Remembered?

As the model shows, the first action in a strategic planning process should be the creation of a *vision*. In his discussion of

visions in *The Seven Habits of Highly Effective People,* author
Stephen Covey suggests thinking of how you or your organization *wants to be remembered.* In this light, the vision should be
long term and should address what the company or individual
ultimately wants to become. A company should think five to ten
years out, asking itself: If we could design the "perfect" situation
ten years from now, what would this company look like?

Each company or individual may have different ideas about
what a vision should contain. The vision should custom fit the
individual or company. But certain elements are common to all
visions:

1. It should be relatively brief and written in future
    tense.
2. It should be based on an analysis of the company's
    current status and goals.
3. It should be believed and disseminated from the top
    of the organization.
4. It should set the long-term direction of the entire
    company.
5. It should be able to be internalized by all.

What a Vision is Not

The description above seems succinct, uncomplicated, and
to the point, doesn't it? However, you would be surprised at
how many *visions* are really *missions.* The key difference is that
a mission contains no long-term thinking. Many of the visions
I've read do include some of the elements above, but they are
so lengthy and cumbersome that stakeholders cannot "connect"
with the vision. If those who are supposed to be striving toward

a vision cannot embrace it, the vision will lack credibility and will not encourage people to action and improvement.

It is also readily evident that many so-called visions are simply catch phrases or clusters of motivational sayings meant to inspire those already toiling on a daily basis to toil even harder, without clearly addressing the purpose of their efforts.

An example of this in daily life would be a family going on vacation and deciding when they are going to leave, but never deciding on a destination. They are all excited and happy. They get in their car, but after a few days of traveling with no idea of where they are going, they begin to get a bit frustrated. The same frustration will happen in an organization without clear direction.

Analysis is Key

To customize a vision to the particular concerns of an organization, the vision must be based on a thorough analysis of the company's infrastructure. Leadership books abound with analysis techniques. Three of the best analysis techniques I've found are:

1. SWOT – an acronym derived from analyzing a company's **S**trengths, **W**eaknesses, **O**pportunities, and **T**hreats
2. Beliefs Audit – analyzing a company's core values
3. Stakeholder Analysis – identifying any person or group who will be affected in any way by the organization.

These three kinds of analyses make the planners think about whom they serve, what they believe, and what they need to do to become the very best they can be. In writing your vision, before you can plan where you ultimately want to go, you need to analyze where you have been and where you are at present. It is extremely important for the primary leader to be involved in this vision-setting process, because if the leader doesn't totally agree and buy into the vision, the strategic plan will not succeed.

After many years of developing plans using these analysis tools, I have learned the importance of each and how to use them in the successful design of a strategic plan.

S.W.O.T.

By using chart pads and group interaction, the facilitator can quickly gather input and insight into the organization for which he/she is helping develop a plan for improvement. The strengths and weaknesses are generally internal points of reference while the opportunities and threats are generally external. Once this exercise is completed and the input is displayed in a place of prominence, the planners can use the input when developing the vision and mission as well as the goals and objectives. Once the plan is completed, it is especially helpful to check how many of the weaknesses should be an area of emphasis in the final plan development.

It will be interesting and quite acceptable to find some of the same issues coming up as both areas of strength as well as areas of weakness. Often a specific example often times comes from staffing issues. Some may say the stability of staff is a strength while some may say that same stability is a weakness. This seeming conflict is fine at this stage of the input process because both conclusions may be correct.

It is imperative to let all who want input to have an opportunity to do so. No judgements of right or wrong are allowed in this process.

Beliefs Audit

The beliefs audit is a straightforward activity that helps those in the strategic planning process gain an insight into what they and their organization believe about what and why their organization exists and what their organization attempts to do for the client(s). When completing this analysis tool, I usually just start with a blank chart pad and write at the top, "We believe…" Then we just begin to fill in the thoughts of those in the group planning process. The results of this analysis technique provides a very simple and an applicable way to develop goal statements. Most often there is a direct correlation between the beliefs audit and what the group believes they must do to make their organization better.

It is important to allow each participant to have input, even though some disagreement may exist. What will normally happen is that the facilitator can group some of the beliefs into goal statements and include most everyone's idea or at least lead the group to consensus on priorities.

Stakeholder Analysis

In order to make this analysis, the facilitator will make another chart. On this chart the group will list any person or group affected by the operations of this organization. Again this is a straightforward technique to get the group thinking about who they serve and why. A simple list of all people and groups affected by the operation gives a framework for the thought process of plan development. When the plan is finished as well as while it is being developed, this list of stakeholders gives structure and direction for those developing the plan. Once the plan is thought to be complete, the facilitator can bring the group back to this list and ask how many of their identified stakeholders have been addressed in the plan. This serves as a check on the completeness of the plan.

It is imperative to allow the group developing the plan to think beyond the four walls of the organization. It is amazing how many ideas for improvement and even business expansion can come out of this single technique.

Start Your Engines!

As I write this chapter of the book, it is May in Indiana. Naturally, many Hoosiers are excitedly anticipating the Indianapolis 500. Let's imagine a young driver coming up the ranks of open-wheel racing. He is serious about making a career of racing. With this in mind, let's help this driver establish a strategic plan for his career.

> **VISION:** *I will become the next great Indianapolis 500 race driver and be remembered as one of the best race drivers of all time.*

With the vision in place, the next step in the process is to establish the mission.

Mission: Focusing on Present Tense

Just what exactly is a *mission?* A mission is what an individual, organization, or company is about today. It answers the question, "On a daily basis, what do I (or what does the organization/company) actually do?" Like the vision, the mission should be fairly short in length, easy to remember, and easy to embrace. All too often, however, I've seen missions that are paragraphs long and cumbersome. Full of well-intentioned statements, they miss the mark of what a true mission should express: the ongoing, daily activities of the company. The mission should flow logically into the vision. The pivotal thought is this: "If I fulfill my mission daily, I will ultimately achieve my vision."

Keep It Specific

Much of the work entailed in establishing a vision can be used in establishing a mission. This includes the analysis of the company's purpose. However, the mission's focus is of shorter term and should be more specific. It reflects the process from vision to objectives; i.e., going from very general to very specific principles. The mission should also be reevaluated each time the strategic planning process takes place, whether semiannually or annually or even more often.

While the vision is expressed in future-oriented language, the mission should be in present tense. It should reflect where the company, individual, or organization is today, not where it wants to be.

Let's look at our race driver's mission and see if it meets the criteria above.

MISSION: *I am an open-wheel racer who is practicing, competing, and learning about my sport each day, continuing to improve my skills as a racing driver on my way to participating in the Indianapolis 500.*

The questions we must now ask are these: If this driver continues to fulfill his mission, can he ultimately fulfill the vision? Does this mission logically flow into the vision? If it does, then it is an acceptable mission.

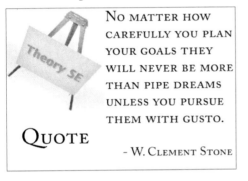

NO MATTER HOW CAREFULLY YOU PLAN YOUR GOALS THEY WILL NEVER BE MORE THAN PIPE DREAMS UNLESS YOU PURSUE THEM WITH GUSTO.

QUOTE

- W. CLEMENT STONE

Goals: Aiming for Success

After the company has established its mission, it needs to direct its attention to setting *goals*. When facilitating this process with companies, I encourage them to avoid being overly aggressive the first time through in determining goals. Establishing three to five goals during the first planning session is sufficient to activate the mission and move it toward achieving the vision. The goals should flow logically from the mission and be in line with the analyses completed earlier during the vision planning session. Goals should be based on the corporation or individual's areas of need or emphasis. Achieving the goals will enable the organization or individual to continuously improve, fulfill the mission, and move toward the vision. Many times when helping a company establish goals, I use the results of the beliefs audit to custom fit the goals to the company's mission. Basing goals upon core beliefs is not only a natural progression but is also quite logical and pragmatic.

Let's return to our Indy driver. During the beliefs audit, he made this statement, "I believe that to be a 500 champion, you must 'pay my dues' coming up." We can assume the driver has been "paying dues" for some time and is ready to take the next step toward the vision. If that is the case, we can phrase a goal as follows:

GOAL: *I believe I can pass my rookie test.*

As you have probably already surmised, the next question is this: If the driver fulfills this goal, will that help to fulfill the mission which, in turn, will ultimately help to achieve the vision?

If so, the goal is acceptable. If not, the goal should be revised to make sure it *does* flow logically. If the goal is acceptable, the next step is to create objectives to help reach the goal.

Objectives: Measuring Success

Objectives are the real meat of the plan. The objectives describes the action necessary to complete the goal. Items which will be evaluated to determine progress. Establishing objectives involves setting guidelines or rules, just like we did when conducting the vision, mission, and goal-setting sessions of strategic planning. When I facilitate this process with companies and organizations, I try to form a template that can be used through the entire process.

In building objectives, I look at two aspects. First, I gener-

ally preface each objective with something like this: "I (we) will
... (action to take place)." Second, I establish a timeline, clearly
indicating how long the objective will take to complete.

These two parts, the action and the timeline, give a concrete
way to evaluate whether or not the objective has been met. That
is the single most important aspect of the objective. It *must* be
measurable. We do not just say an objective has or has not been
completed. We ask, "What are the specific measurements of
success?"

Just as I encourage companies to avoid being overly aggressive in establishing goals, I also encourage them to be a bit con-
servative in establishing objectives. Usually three to five objectives for each goal are plenty to handle the first time through the
strategic planning process.

Creating more objectives than can reasonably be accomplished may cause the planners to become frustrated and sense
failure. On the other hand, the objectives should stretch the
company as well as the individuals in the company to move
towards the fulfillment of the stated goal.

In looking at our driver's goal, let's set some specific, measurable objectives for him to achieve in order to attain that goal
... which will help to fulfill the mission ... which will help to
achieve the vision.

OBJECTIVES:

1. By June 1, I will obtain a full-time ride for the
   remainder of the race season.
2. I will qualify and participate in four IRL races
   before May 1, of the next calendar year.
3. I will test at Indy in October of the present season.

Now come the inevitable questions: Are the objectives specific and measurable? Will accomplishing these objectives help the driver achieve the goal, which will help to fulfill the mission, which will ultimately help to achieve the vision? If the answers are yes, the objectives are acceptable, if no they need to be refined.

Summary: Standardize the Vision

The first of the tripod braces is the strategic planning brace. This chapter's discussion has underlined the importance of strategic planning in helping to strengthen the *Leadership Tripod*. Without a plan, leadership flounders. With a plan, leadership has direction and focus. For organizations, companies, families, or a leader's personal life, the significance of effective planning cannot be overstated.

If sub-organizations within a larger organization create their own strategic plans, these plans need to flow logically into the larger organization's strategic plan. Each goal and objective should meld with and assist in achieving the corporate vision. In fact, when facilitating the strategic planning process, I always urge subgroups to keep the same vision as the larger group.

Maintain Perspective

After having facilitated and carried out many strategic plans and processes, I have one final suggestion for those wishing to begin this process. Do not use an in-house person to facilitate the strategic planning process. Someone outside the company or organization will have a much more objective approach, will see the company through an unbiased lens, and will have the impartiality necessary to give a fair and candid appraisal. However, it is important for the facilitator to be knowledgeable about strategic planning, thus avoiding overextension of the process. As I mentioned earlier in this chapter, taking too long and spending too much will hinder rather than improve the company's chances of establishing a viable strategic plan. Remember, a good facilitator also has a mission. The facilitator will skillfully pursue that mission to create an environment conducive to the strategic planning process and to aggressively expedite the process—for the good of all involved.

It is also important for the facilitator to meet with the leaders of the company and other stakeholders before the planning session begins. The facilitator should be as knowledgeable as possible of the history and intricacies of the organization.

Plan Building Exercise

1. Do I know my company's vision and mission? Does what I do on a daily basis help to fulfill the vision and mission? If not, why not? (If your company has a vision and a mission, write them below.)

2. If you have a vision for your own life, write it below. If you don't have one, begin the creation process by completing a beliefs audit and SWOT analysis, then begin your vision.

3. If you have a mission for your life, write it below. If you don't have one, begin the creation process by writing down some thoughts for your mission.

4. List at least three of your company's goals, or list three goals for yourself or your family. Be sure these contribute to the achievement of your vision and mission. Use your beliefs audit as a guide.

5. List at least two measurable objectives for each of the goals. Be sure to address weaknesses from the SWOT analysis.

Note:

Use the strategic plans in Appendix I as a reference if you need further clarification.

1 Ken Blanchard, Bill Hybels, and Phil Hodges, *Leadership by the Book: Tools to Transform Your Workplace* (New York: William Morrow andCo., 1999), 55.

2 A full-time ride means a driver is part of a fully funded IRL (Indy Racing League) team for a complete season of racing.

CHAPTER 4

BRACED ON ACCORD
COMMUNICATION

Communication

Although the strategic plan helps to stabilize the tripod, one brace is not enough to ensure structural stability. As you can see in the Tripod diagram, we still need two more braces to make the tripod as strong as it can be. This chapter will focus on the second brace, *Communication*.

The Big "C"

Over the years, what I have found is that people complain a lot either about communication in general or the lack of effective communication in an organization/company/family. However, few do anything *but* complain. During this discussion of communication, I will not only try to give general principles of effective communication, but I will also to give specifics on how to improve and evaluate the communication in an organization. My premise is straightforward: *leadership will not be as strong as it should be in order for the organization to achieve at its highest level without effective communication.*

A couple of years ago I referred to "The Big 'C'" in one of my articles.[1] The focus of my article was the misconception about communication. It is my opinion that most of those who complain about a lack of communication view it to be a one-way passing of information from the top down to those under leadership, or from the leader on up to those who place leaders. If either end of the spectrum believes this to be the case, communication will always be an exercise in frustration. That is why everyone in an organization needs to have a better understanding about what communication actually is and what their role is in making sure effective communication takes place.

Misconceptions

To say that effective communication is important in creating a healthy corporation, family, or organization is to state the obvious. However, there is currently not much real analysis of communication problems or specific solutions designed to enhance and improve communication for both internal and external customers.

I also see far too many top-level executives clinging tightly to the "one-way" interpretation of communication, while those being led have a completely different perception. I recently asked a vice president of an organization how he would rate his organization's lines of communication. His answer spoke volumes.

JUST REALIZING COMMUNICATIONS ARE AN ISSUE IS NOT ENOUGH. A SYSTEMATIC METHOD OF IMPROVED COMMUNICATIONS MUST BE ESTABLISHED.

TIP

He answered, "Oh, they're great! We send communications to all our staff all the time." His perception was that if he sent out information on a regular basis, he was "communicating."

Most of his staff didn't share that same perception. They told me that although they were being sent "stuff," no one was really communicating with them.

The same misunderstanding about communication is true if viewed from the perspective of the leader. Many leaders feel the very ones they are trying to lead don't communicate with them. They may assert that they believe in an "open door" policy, but wonder why no one feels free to come through the "open door."

These common misconceptions about communication require specific kinds of intervention in order to create a shared perception.

If the leader wants people to come through his or her door, then the leader may have to go out of the door of the office first and onto the floor of the manufacturing facility or wherever the stakeholders are. This action may be necessary before the staff feels enough trust and comfort to go through the "open door" of the leader.

Defining Communication

Essentially, communication is the passing of information between at least two parties. This can take many forms, as I will attempt to explain in this chapter. In my experience, communication only becomes effective when both parties understand what the communication was designed to accomplish.

To say it another way, for communication to take place, someone must create it (encode it) and then someone must receive it (decode it). Between the time a communication is encoded and the time it is decoded, many things can and often do happen. Some authors refer to an interruption in the flow of the communication as "noise."

The Effect of Noise

This "noise" can take many forms. This disruption can actually can be noise as we know it. For example, those attending a NASCAR race would have trouble communicating verbally during the race. The noise of the engines would cause the decoder not to understand the encoded message resulting in, no communication.

Noise can also refer to the emotions of the encoder or decoder. Let's say that a leader is trying to communicate an important message to a stakeholder. Just before this communication, the stakeholder had learned of a family tragedy. The emotions of the stakeholder may cause the decoder to ignore or misinterpret the encoded message

I'm familiar with this kind of noise. Last term I was teaching an MBA class which was the last class the students had to pass before they graduated. I had explained the requirements of the class and time lines for completion to the students. Late in the course a student told me she wouldn't be able to complete her final assignment. I was a little irritated (to say the least) because it was evident she hadn't "heard" what I had encoded to her about the requirements for the course. I proceeded to "tell" her again that she would indeed complete the assignment if she intended to graduate, and I would accept no excuses. After repeatedly trying to break through the "noise" of my irritation, she finally managed to encode her message in a way that I could decode it. Her son had been convicted of felony murder two days earlier and her son's circumstances precluded her ability to complete the assignment on time. Once we both cleared the air of emotional noise, we were able to decode what the other was saying and come to a solution to the problem. Before commu-

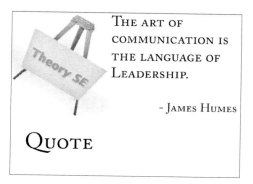

THE ART OF COMMUNICATION IS THE LANGUAGE OF LEADERSHIP.

- JAMES HUMES

QUOTE

nication could take place, we each had to get past our respective emotional noise. If we had not been able to silence the noise, we could both have failed in our attempts to communicate. Then both our visions; mine of being a good professor and hers of being a graduate, would have failed.

I was recently watching a TV commercial for cell phones. The actor in the ad made a very profound statement: "Isn't communication great when it works?" Many times, noise can damage communication or even render it worthless. The actor was referring to actual noise which hindered the transmission of the message through the cell phone. Sometimes what one person says is not always what the other person hears. Such was the case in the commercial. For true communication to take place, the receiver has to be able to decode the message the way the encoder intended for it to be understood.

The Missing Link

While very basic, the model below demonstrates the key principles for effective communication. In order to be sure a message has been decoded correctly, there needs to be some link back to the one who originally encoded the message. Without that link, how does one know the communication has been received and understood the way it was intended?

Methods

Encoding ————————————————→ Decoding

↑   (Noise)   ↓

Decoding ←———————————————— Encoding

To repeat and important concept, I see too many leaders and those under leadership just *assuming* communication has taken place and then getting upset when they find it hasn't. Both need to take the time to create a process that will systematically check to see if communication has been successful. This process will save those encoding and those decoding much frustration. This 360 degree feedback is essential in being assured that communication has taken place.

One entity encoding information without a corresponding entity decoding the information is NOT communication. But, sadly, this is exactly what happens in many companies, organizations, and even families.

The CEO sends a memo to everyone that the staff must be reduced as a cost cutting measure to save the company from going out of business. The CEO is encoding this communication as a positive way to save the company. The staff decodes (hears) the message that those at the top of the organization just want more money and will sacrifice employees to accomplish the goal of lining their pockets with cash.

The same failure to decode communication accurately can take place at home. The father says: "Son be home by 10pm. No excuses!" He does this because he cares about his son and wants no harm to come to him. The son decodes (hears) "Dad doesn't trust me and is trying to control my life."

These are both common communication break downs caused by emotional noise and lack of clarification. The result of both these scenarios is a misunderstanding of the intended message. Both could be rectified, or at least softened, by taking the time to be sure the circle of the communication chain has been completed. A face to face discussion with stakeholders to explain the specifics of the need to cut staff and the ramifications of doing it and not doing it explained, may not make workers happy, but they may at least understand the decision. Dad telling his son he loves him and that is why he cares enough to set boundaries may not make the son happy about the curfew, but at least might give the son a better understanding of why his father makes the decision he does.

How We Communicate

Let us take a closer look at specific methods of communication, as well as some of the problems that can inhibit the decoding of information.

Verbal Communication

The majority of the time, whether in our family life or business/organizational life, we communicate verbally. Speaking verbally to one another is a direct and effective method of getting messages across. You might think that very little noise would get in the way of a face-to-face communication between the encoder and the decoder. While for the most part this is true, problems can still occur. All members of an organization need to understand what these problems are and how to address them. In the area of verbal communication, the two primary problems are the use of the vernacular and the affect of inflection.

Vernacular: It's Greek to Me!

Many times the words we use in the workplace do not translate well to others outside the workplace. This happens when

we use acronyms, abbreviations, or "legalese" that those outside our business cannot understand. Therefore, while we may
encode in a manner that we understand, the listener may not be
able to decode what we
are saying. For example,
people with limited
computer knowledge
have only to talk to an
authentic computer
"geek" to know what I
mean.

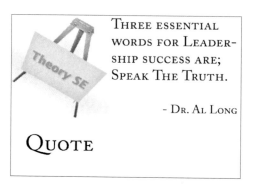

THREE ESSENTIAL
WORDS FOR LEADER-
SHIP SUCCESS ARE;
SPEAK THE TRUTH.

- DR. AL LONG

QUOTE

Recently, I was
making a presentation to a national health care facility group.
We were talking about making decisions and how to implement
a logical decision-making process. When I asked them to give
me a problem to use as an example, they came up with "Plan B
Patients" and their effect on the company. They all knew exactly
what they were talking about, but I didn't have a clue.

In this kind of situation, a listener (decoder) many times is
too embarrassed to admit that he or she doesn't understand what
is being communicated. The listener may also simply decide in
his or her own mind what is meant based on his/her knowledge
base. Both cases are disastrous to effective communication. In
my situation, I asked everyone to back up and explain what
"Plan B Patients" were and why these patients were problematic
to the company. Once we all came to the same understanding,
communication had taken place, and we were able to get on with
solving the problem in a logical manner. We took the TIME to
be sure the decoding was what the encoder had intended.

Inflection: Say That Again?

Many times *how* one says something many times is just as important as *what* one says. The encoder and the decoder may be saying and hearing two very different messages simply because of the way the words are verbalized. An obvious form of this problem occurs when the media edits recorded interviews to attain just the right number of sound bites for the evening news. By carefully editing the recorded words, technology can make someone sound as if he or she is encoding one message when, in fact, the speaker may have meant the message to be decoded in an entirely different manner.

Inflection can also be an excellent tool in effective communication. By varying or modulating the pitch and volume of one's spoken words, a person can make a lasting impression on an audience. Inflection can vitalize words when presented with emotion, or mute them if muttered tonelessly. The same words spoken with different inflections can say very different things to the listener Since we don't have a way to give auditory examples in the text of a book, let's preface a simple sentence with an explanation and then, through punctuation, see if we can simulate the significance of inflection.

Preface: You are a supervisor in a manufacturing setting and you need to communicate verbally to someone under your supervision that cleanliness in the work area is a concern. The message you want to convey is that the area needs to be cleaned: You might say, "You need to clean up around here." Surely anyone can understand that, right? Here are various scenarios of how that message is decoded by the listener:

- **"YOU** need to clean up around here!!!!"
    Spoken in a loud voice, the emphasis is on the word *you*. The decoder will decode the message to mean that he or she needs to do the cleaning.
- "You need to clean up around **HERE**."
    The decoder will probably interpret this to mean that he or she is to clean the specific location of their conversation.
- "You **NEED** to clean up around here."
    The decoder may feel that the encoder is putting pressure on the supervisor to see that the area is cleaned.
- "You need to **CLEAN UP** around here."
    The decoder may feel that the encoder is questioning the decoder's personal hygiene, telling him or her to have cleaner personal habits while at the workplace?

This example demonstrates how inflection can influence the message the decoder is hearing. The encoder needs to be sure that what he or she is trying to convey is what the employee is hearing, so that the employees understands the verbal message the way it was intended.

The Telephone: A Unique Hybrid

The telephone, somewhere between verbal and nonverbal communication, is also a powerful, versatile, and necessary means of communication. With the addition of the cell phone, every leader is at the disposal of anyone who happens to have his or her cell phone number. While this allows you to stay in touch with the office at all times, it also means you are unable to totally get away from the office. When a leader carries a cell phone, the office is wherever he or she might be when the phone rings.

Who Answers the Phone? An often-overlooked aspect of a company or organization's "face" to the world is how it handles its phone communication. Is your company's receptionist responsible for answering the phone or does the company use an automated answering service? When someone calls your company, does the receptionist make a favorable impression on the caller? Does he or she convey professionalism and courtesy?

If your company uses an automated service, is it user-friendly, or is the caller impersonally shuffled from one extension to another, forced to listen to a veritable litany of options? Both verbally and non verbally, the telephone can either improve or sabotage effective communication.

A company must decide the value of someone answering the phone. I know that economically it may make sense to automate, but a significant study should be done before the decision is made. Saving money on a person answering the phone may cost client satisfaction. This decision should be one that is assessed carefully.

A personal example of how customer frustration can cost an organization the loss of a good customer, happened recently in my own home. We had sent a check to finish paying off our mortgage and had never received notice that the mortgage company had received our payment. When my wife, usually a very patient person, called the mortgage company to check on their receipt of our payment, she was systematically shuffled through different people for one full hour! By the time she got to the right person, all hope of that company getting any more of our business was lost, and she told them so. A good customer became a former customer.

To check your own system, you might want to call in as a customer yourself and see what happens. Our own CEO did this just the other day and found that it took him several tries before he could reach the necessary person. This was NOT acceptable and our company made the changes necessary to streamline the process.

Voice Mail: Even if you can't answer the phone right away, most people now have voice mail. Voice mail greatly enhances communication, but comes with problems as well. When used properly voice mail can be a great asset and time saver. When used improperly, it can be frustrating and time consuming. My new catch phrase is "voice mail illiterate." What I have found is that many people just don't know how to use voice mail. For example, let's say you leave this voice mail message: "This is Greg, call me."

What if the person you were calling doesn't recognize your voice? What if that person knows ten men named Greg with ten different phone numbers? Will the recipient take the time to go through that list of ten names? If the caller's original intention was to talk business, what kind of impression will the message leave in the recipient's mind? Will the recipient think the caller is irritated? What will the recipient think of the way the caller is representing the business?

Leaders need to be sure they understand how to leave a message that not only conveys professionalism, but also puts their companies/organizations in a professional light.

Written Communication

The idea of a handwritten note or letter seems almost archaic in today's technology-based society! The phrase "snail mail" seems to sum up this generation's emphasis on rapid communication and immediate feedback. But handwritten notes and letters are still very valuable forms of communication. Other "traditional" forms of written communication include memos, directives, and business letters. More contemporary forms of written communication include E-mail and fax messages.

Handwritten Messages: The Personal Touch

The Note: Whatever your position in the company, the handwritten note of encouragement and affirmation is a powerful tool. It communicates that you have a genuine interest in the one receiving the note (Theory SE). This is especially meaningful in light of today's hectic pace and many demands on your time. Taking the time to write a note of encouragement is a powerful way to communicate a positive message to the addressee..

Problem: The primary problem with this form of communication is one of expectation. If you write a note to one person, others will expect a note from you. The additional burden placed upon the note-writer can outweigh the positive results of the notes themselves.

For example, let's say you're a leader in a company. You've noticed that a certain employee has spent extra non-paid time to complete a project. You handwrite a personal note thanking this person for his or her dedication in completing an important task. However, another employee, one you haven't noticed, has spent just as many or even more hours on the same task. But you don't write this person a note. The inadvertent communication this person receives is that his or her work must not be as valuable as the other employee's work. Even though the leader never intended to communicate this kind of message, that is what the second worker decoded because he or she did not receive a handwritten note.

The Letter: The personal letter is another nearly lost form of written communication. I personally believe letters—handwritten or typed—are important communication vehicles that many leaders fail to utilize, especially in sales and marketing. The follow-up letter can be a very significant part of the sales process. By this I do NOT mean a "canned" set of follow-up letters! I know some leaders who think that once an appointment has been completed, all they have to do is hit a key on their computers and print out a form letter designed for the occasion. They consider the "canned" letter that the printer spews out to be sufficient thanks to a client or potential client for the time spent at the appointment. As one who has received these kinds of letter, I can personally attest that they are NOT effective. A personally written letter and one kicked out of a database are worlds apart. I am especially impressed when I receive a letter that mentions specific things we talked about in our meeting. Such letters don't have to be handwritten, but when they are, the impact is even more significant. A personal letter make valuable deposits into the emotional bank account of stakeholders—especially in times of grief, celebration, weddings, graduations, and other special occasions in the lives of the letter recipients.

Problem: As with handwritten notes, the sheer volume of letters a person would have to compose could be overwhelming.

However, even canned letters can be personalized. If nothing else, jot a quick P.S. on the bottom of the letter. This at least lets the decoder know that the encoder was personally involved with the letter; he or she didn't just ask an assistant to mail a "canned" response.

Electronic Mail: First it was the fax machine, an electronic convenience that is still a major component of the technology revolution. Next, E-mail has become the communication of choice. E-mail is easy, quick, and efficient. E-mail saves time and resources. With E-mail there are no envelopes to lick, and no stamps to purchase. E-mail is faster, less cumbersome, and more private than the fax machine. Those needing to meet pressing deadlines can even send documents as E-mail attachments. Feedback is almost immediate.

Problem: E-mail's assets are also its greatest problems. It's easy, it's quick, it's efficient . . . or is it? Typing a quick E-mail and sending it off into cyberspace seems to rid the encoder of responsibility for making sure the communication has been received and decoded the way it was intended. This has happened to me. On occasion I've asked people why they didn't communicate with me as we had agreed. The response? "I sent you an E-mail. Didn't you get it?" Having met their obligation to communicate, they felt it was then up to me, the receiver, to notify them if the E-mail didn't get through.

A second problem with E-mail is that it is impersonal. Many use E-mail as a shield to keep from having to confront an audience verbally, either face-to-face or by phone. It seems to be much easier to complain, attack, or belittle by E-mail than it is to meet personally and talk over the situation.

Finally, there is an inherent danger of decoding emotion in an E-mail that was not intended or misreading the intent of the communication.

Nonverbal Communication

Authors have written books on nonverbal communication. Nonverbal communication or how we convey messages through body language, gestures, facial expressions, behaviors, our sense of personal space—even what we drive, how we dress, and whom we hang out with—is a field ripe for analysis and debate. Obviously, I cannot even scratch the surface, except to underscore the importance of nonverbal communication in our everyday interactions. Many times these nonverbal clues are the most overlooked and yet most obvious factor in determining miscommunication.

Let me use a NASCAR race as an example. The points leader for the championship needed to make a pit stop. Another veteran driver was following him. The first driver motioned his intentions with his left hand and proceeded to pull to the bottom of the track. The first driver thought he had encoded his nonverbal message clearly. However, the second driver decoded the nonverbal message as a direction for him to move to the bottom of the track. The result of this nonverbal miscommunication was a huge wreck. In corporate, business, or family life, nonverbal miscommunication can often have disastrous results.

Problem: Essentially, the problem with nonverbal communication is that few people even realize the messages they are sending a nonverbal message. A candidate who is fidgeting during a job interview may be completely unaware of this nervous reaction. However, the interviewer, who is trying to select a PR spokesperson for the company, may bypass this candidate, based on the nonverbal communication alone. I encourage leaders and potential leaders to take the time to study nonverbal communication and incorporate this knowledge into your organization. Used properly, nonverbal communication can be a positive and powerful dynamic in leadership training.

Summary

This chapter only scratches the surface regarding the significance of communication and the varieties and forms of communication available today. We didn't touch on electronic meetings, pagers, marketing materials, and a host of other communication options coming into vogue. Hopefully, you have seen how strong the brace of communications needs to be to support effective leadership. Without an effective communication process in place, those involved in leadership cannot be as productive as they should be. Communication, along with strategic planning, has to be an integral part of any organization if that organization is to realize success. Success cannot and will not just "happen." An organization doesn't improve by accident. It needs careful attention and consistent maintenance to be the very best it can be for both internal and external customers.

Self-Assessment Exercise

1. The communication in our organization is:
    a. Excellent
    b. Good
    c. Average
    d. Below Average
    e. Poor

    If your answer is c, d, or e, why do you believe
    that to be the case?
    How will you address the problem?
    If your answer is a or b, why do you believe
    this to be the case?
    How can you verify your answer?

2. The communication in our family is?

3. How do you know effective communication is taking
    place in your organization and in your family?

4. Do you spend adequate time training leaders and staff in
    effective communication techniques?

5. Do you have a specific method to assess the effectiveness
    of all forms of communication in your area of responsi-
    bility for effectiveness?

6. What will be your first act in evaluating and improving
    your personal communication techniques?

Case Scenario

You are the leader of an organization. You have facilities in four different locations and your headquarters is not adjacent to any of them. You do have e-mail capabilities but you cannot get all stakeholders together in one place at one time.

You have been informed by your Chief Financial Officer that although you have just received notification of the acceptance of a significant new contract, this contract will not be bringing in revenue for 18 months. You are now strapped for cash flow and you do not currently have enough work to keep all your staff productive. How will you communicate the seeming contradiction of good news about the contract and the bad news about being laid off?

1. First, list the information you must communicate to your staff?

2. What are the first five things about this communication that came to your mind?

3. How will you make this communication to all your staff?

4. What kinds of alternative actions do you believe you could incorporate?

[1]   A. Long, "Administrative Shortage: Perception/Reality/Solutions," *IPLA Special Edition* 13 (May 2000): 3.

CHAPTER **5**

BRACED ON PRINCIPLE
MORALS/ETHICS

Morals/Ethics

The last brace stabilizing the leadership tripod is *Morals and Ethics*. Please understand that I do not mean to impose my personal code of ethics on you, the reader. I want to underscore the importance of the moral and ethical brace in sustaining a company's overall health and stability. Moral and ethical behavior should be modeled by leadership at all levels—in leaders themselves, in those who select leaders, and in those under leadership.

However, it is not just enough to model these key traits. One leader's interpretation of what is ethical behavior may differ from another's in alarming ways. Consequently, the organization needs a baseline from which to operate.

Establishing the Baseline

Honesty, respect, cooperation, and integrity are character traits or core beliefs which are common to most businesses, schools, or other organizations. A company or organization needs to establish its own set of core beliefs or values in order to gauge its purpose, progress, and success. These values should be the road map the company uses to make all its ethical and moral decisions.

Some examples of a company's set of values for ethical behavior might be:

- No gifts accepted over X dollars
- No alcohol at company functions
- No layoffs
- No puffery in advertising
- Timely payment of all vendors.

When everyone in an organization understands what is and is not acceptable company behavior, everyone also clearly understands the boundaries within which they are expected to operate. Understanding the boundaries means there is no room for individual interpretation of the company's ethical and moral standards.

What's the Bottom Line?

We've all heard stories about unethical business practices and corporations with the reputations for being "shark tanks." The media seems to revel in uncovering the latest corporate scandals. With that in mind, it's no surprise that much research has focused on the ethical practices of companies and organizations. What might surprise you, however, are the results of these studies. Over the long term, companies that operate morally and ethically outperform those that don't. In looking at profit, the unethical firms may take a short-term lead, but that lead evaporates over time.

Let's look at the *Leadership Tripod* again, and imagine that great boulder bearing down on the top piece. As we saw earlier, the tripod may stand for a while, but eventually it will collapse from the strain. Without braces, the legs will buckle. And it is my opinion that the most important brace of all is the Moral and Ethical brace. It must be the strongest.

> **TIP**
>
> ESTABLISH A SET OF BELIEFS FOR THE ORGANIZATION. IT MUST BE MODELED AND DISSEMINATED FROM THE TOP DOWN.

But how do you know that this brace is as strong as it should be? How do you judge whether people in your business are operating morally and ethically? Or whether they are making moral and ethical decisions? Do you gauge this by the company's bottom line or by the company's retention rate, or by the attendance rate, or by the pay scale, or because your husband or wife says so?

My contention is that leadership needs to have a concrete *method* by which to judge whether or not their companies and those working in those companies are operating according to the company's established core beliefs.

I was once told that to judge whether or not you are acting in a moral and ethical manner is to ask yourself the question, "If 60 Minutes came into my office today, how would I face Mike Wallace and answer his questions"? If this thought sends chills down your spine, you probably have ethical and moral problems.

A Personal Model

I recognize that choosing morals and ethics is an area of personal choice and that you are entitled to set your own limits and boundaries. However, I would like to share a model that I use to judge whether decisions I make in my personal or professional life are ethical and moral. Each time I undergo this process, I take time to examine the values that undergird my professional and personal life.

To understand and explain the *Utility-Justice-Rights* model, I will use a real-life example. We will use the example of an entrepreneur who has decided to buy and renovate houses, and then resell them or rent them. This type of business causes one to automatically look for houses which are bargains, and may not be in the best shape. After laboring to fix these bargain homes for resale or rental, the entrepreneur hopes to make a profit. In this example case, a realtor calls and asks the businesswoman to look at a house going up for absolute auction. Absolute auction means that the house does not have to bring a base price; the highest bid, whatever it is, will be awarded the house. The businesswoman looks at the property, which was part of an estate. To say this house was a mess would be an understatement. The businesswoman's decision would be simple: would she buy the house or not?

One might wonder how buying this house could present a moral and ethical dilemma. The moral and ethical dilemma became apparent when the businesswoman used the *utility-justice-rights* process in order to come to make her decision about buying the house.

Here is what the businesswoman realized as she filtered her decision through the model. Note that there is no chronological order to the steps below. You may wish to arrange your model differently—just remember to examine all three points carefully.

Utility

Utilitarianism means, simply, do the benefits outweigh the costs? In this case, the businesswoman had to decide whether or not she would benefit financially by buying this house and reselling and/or renting it. The businesswoman knew that she could probably rent the house to a renter just the way it was. After all, people had been living in it, so people could live in it again. If she obtained the house at a good price, and didn't have to pay for any renovation, she could then justify the purchase of the home based solely on Utility. Her benefit of collecting rent on the house would outweigh her financial liability in purchasing it.

This is the way many companies, leaders, and even those under leadership make decisions. They look to see if the benefits of a decision outweigh the costs, and then they go full speed ahead with their decision. Considering only the financial bottom line can have disastrous results.

An example of this kind of decision making is a company that makes staffing decisions based on the doctrine of utility. Let's say the company lays off many of its employees. The short-term result, of course, is a ballooning of the bottom line. However, this short-term result will be eclipsed by the company's long-term failure to anticipate the real costs of the lay off—a loss of seasoned employees responsible for the efficient operation of the company's day-to-day business. This decision based on utility will come back to haunt the leaders who made the decision. This could happen in the case scenario from the earlier chapter.

Justice

There are three kinds of justice—egalitarian, distributive, and retributive.

Egalitarian Justice

Egalitarian justice determines if you are treating all stakeholders equally. In deciding whether to buy the house, the businesswoman now could, with full confidence, say this purchase is not an egalitarian justice issue. So, she was OK according to egalitarian justice.

In the organizational setting, leaders need to be certain they are treating their employees in a fair and equal manner. For example, in deciding employee fringe benefits, the issue for egalitarian justice is not that the dollar amount for each employee has to be the same. Treating employees equally means treating those in similar job positions equitably. If a leader makes decisions "on a whim" or plays favorites, those decisions are not moral and ethical under the doctrine of egalitarianism.

Distributive Justice

Distributive justice asks the question, "Are you giving out what the others are giving in?" In the case of the businesswoman who buys and rents houses, this question would be phrased, "Is she going to charge rent on a reasonable basis for what the house is worth?" A second question might be phrased, "Is she going to be able to purchase the house for what she thinks it is worth?" And still another, "Can she get out of the house what she would have to put into it?" Under the doctrine of distributive justice, the businesswoman has some problems.

First, she could probably get the house for a low price. But then the question becomes would she be able to charge enough rent to compensate herself for what she would need to invest in the house to bring it up to livable standards? The answer to this would probably be no.

Second, she could rent it out "as-is", but whatever she charged for rent would probably not measure up to the doctrine of distributive justice. Those paying money to live in the house would not be getting the value they deserved for their money.

In reality, at this point the businesswoman would realize that this decision does not measure up to her moral and ethical standards and she would probably decide not to buy the house. Since the only way she could make money on this house would be to rent it without making any renovations, the decision to buy this house would not be just. However, for the sake of argument, let's follow the process to its farthest parameters.

Retributive Justice

Retributive justice is exemplified by the understanding that people get what they deserve based on their actions. With this belief some landlords would justify renting out a substandard house. Such a landlord might decide that any family agreeing to rent this house deserves what they get since they are responsible for getting themselves into such a sorry situation. This kind of landlord would feel justified taking their money and letting them live in substandard conditions. Our businesswoman does not believe that anyone deserves to live in a home of sub-standard conditions, so based on this part of the process, she would continue to decide against purchasing this property.

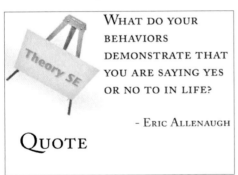

WHAT DO YOUR BEHAVIORS DEMONSTRATE THAT YOU ARE SAYING YES OR NO TO IN LIFE?

- ERIC ALLENAUGH

QUOTE

Even though the businesswoman has already made her decision, let's pretend that somehow she was able to get past the doctrine of justice. There is still yet another measure in this process of testing ethical and moral decisions.

Rights

Two subsections fall under this category: positive rights and negative rights. These can be confusing to some, but they are important considerations in the process of deciding whether a decision is ethical and moral.

Positive rights are quality-of-life issues. If the business-woman were to purchase the house, she would ask herself, "Am I going to positively affect the quality of life of renters who might live in this house?" Of course, her answer would be another resounding NO!

If somehow she could have justified the decision to buy the house under utility and justice, she could never have classified this decision as ethical under the doctrine of positive rights. Renting this house to a renter in its current condition would most assuredly not improve his or her quality of life.

Negative rights are rights that cannot be taken from some-one. These are the constitutional rights of life, liberty, and the pursuit of happiness. If somehow the businesswoman had gotten this far in her decision to buy the house, the doctrine of negative rights would necessitate a decision not to buy the house. Renting out a slum-like house would not enhance the renter's pursuit of happiness.

Summary: Counting the Cost

As you have probably already surmised, I consider the moral and ethical brace a critically important component of the *Leadership Tripod*. Without strong ethics and morals sustaining leadership at any level, success will be short lived. Longevity in leadership relies on a strong ethical and moral foundation. The individual standards, beliefs, and values may differ somewhat from company to company, but they need to be examined and assessed regularly, and they need to be effectively communicated throughout the organization.

Enron's collapse is a prime example of failure in the area of ethics and morals. In 2002 Enron had the sorry distinction of being the largest company ever to fail because of unethical accounting practices. The leaders of the organization were finally called to Washington to defend their behaviors. The ugly truth unearthed was that the leadership had operated in a totally utilitarian mind-set, allowing personal gain to outweigh the costs not only to those under their leadership but also to countless others outside the corporation. The whole flawed structure finally came down upon them, but not before many thousands of people had lost millions of dollars, their jobs, and their retirement funds. Had the leaders and decision-makers of Enron operated from an ethical and moral compass, the company might still be viable today. It does not matter that Enron might, in fact, have had a plan and communicated it effectively, but their unethical behavior caused their collapse.

Self-Assessment Exercise

1. Do you and/or your company have an established set of
    values and have those values been disseminated?

2. When weighing whether a decision is moral and ethical,
    do you filter that decision through a process like the *util-
    ity-justice-rights?*

Case Scenario

Let us reconsider the earlier case scenario regarding the company with a new contract coming in the long term, but a lag of resources for the short term. In this scenario the top decision makers have come to the conclusion that they must lay-off 25% of the work force for at least 12 months. They have also recommended that because of the upcoming contract, no management or leadership positions should be cut.

The recommendation has been made and now you walk into your handsome office to make the final decision. Practice running the decision through the final filter of decision making and explain if you will accept or reject the recommendation of the top decision makers and why.

1. Does this recommendation have utility?
   If so, is the utility so compelling as to stop at this point and make the decision?

2. Is the recommendation just?
   If not just where does it fail? If just, how?

3. Is the recommendation right?

4. What is your final decision?

CHAPTER **6**

FOUNDATIONAL CULTURE
BEHAVIORS AND BELIEFS

Behaviors and Beliefs

How do you solidify leadership? The answer: By establishing and cultivating a solid base of *culture*. I would like the reader to examine the *Leadership Tripod* and imagine the model without the firm base of culture beneath its legs. Even if the legs are structurally sound and the braces are strong, the tripod will function best on a level surface. A photographer working with a tripod often struggles to get his camera in place, just as our "would be" artist did in the parable at the beginning of the book. By adjusting the tripod legs, the photographer can manage to finally achieve enough balance to get the shot he wants. However, this adjustment often places undue stress on the tripod itself. If the photographer is not careful, the entire structure can topple, sending the camera crashing onto the rocks.

The same is true of leadership. Without a level, healthy culture beneath the tripod, leadership will perch precariously upon an unsound structure. Without a strong foundation, effective, long term leadership may be impossible. Short periods of success may fall prey to long periods of problems without a healthy culture. Conversely, leadership can withstand challenges and storms if firmly planted in a healthy culture.

The Components of Culture

Many authors and scholars use the word *climate* interchangeably with *culture*. In defining "climate," *Webster's Dictionary* includes this description: *the prevailing influence or environmental conditions characterizing a group.* Regarding the word "culture," the dictionary says this: *the set of shared attitudes, values, goals, and practices that characterizes a company or corporation.*

I prefer the term *culture* because I think it much more clearly defines the attitudes, emotions, and general *feel* of the organization and its leadership. I also like what Webster's says elsewhere in its definition of culture: *"the act of developing the intellectual and moral faculties . . . expert care and training."* [1]

Climate and culture consultants abound today. These experts have written many articles and books, and regularly conduct climate and culture audits for individuals, businesses, and not for profit organizations. Their primary concern is to focus a company or individual on what to do to foster a healthy corporate environment. As we saw in chapter three, many times these consultants' very fine intentions result in a cumbersome, expensive, and time-consuming process with little to show for the effort. What is really needed is a simple model by which a company can measure the health of its culture and learn to *cultivate the culture* it really wants and needs.

A Lesson from the Bees

When explaining what comprises culture, I like to ask my clients to imagine two bees buzzing around, and then I point to a visual aid with a picture of bees. I tell them to think of these bees as "cultured bees." And then I explain that culture is comprised of two "B's": *behaviors and beliefs.*

In the *Leadership Tripod* model, the behaviors and beliefs sit underneath the culture. Imagine what would happen if the behaviors and beliefs didn't match. All the components of a viable leadership structure would still be in place, but the foundation would no longer be level. And that would skew the structure enough to endanger it, causing leadership to topple and the tripod to collapse. To have a healthy culture, a company and its leaders not only must have a system of beliefs, but they must also behave in a way that matches the beliefs they espouse.

Mixed Messages

Over the years as I have studied success and failure in leadership, I have found one constant that distinguishes those leaders and organizations that succeed from those that fail. Simply put, those who fail do not behave the way they say they believe. This inconsistency causes imbalance in the culture of the organization and sabotages effective leadership. This is not to say, of course, that circumstances beyond control of the organization and/or its leaders can also cause failure. Many times though, an unhealthy culture is the compelling issue to cause organizations to fail.

"Don't do as I do . . ."

Families in chaos reflect this same inconsistency. In working with dysfunctional families, it seldom takes me long to find that the root cause of the problem is in the family's culture. The family's culture is unhealthy because they espouse one set of beliefs but then behave in a totally different manner.

Let's imagine a family in which Mom and Dad have told their children to be honest, to treat others fairly, and to honor commitments. We would call those good core beliefs. Then the children observe Mom and Dad laughing because they did not report all of their income to the IRS. They hear Mom call in sick when she really just wants a day off. They hear Dad whispering on the phone, arranging to meet another woman for dinner. What do you think is going on in the minds of these children?

Because they see a mismatch of beliefs and behaviors, they do not have a healthy culture—a solid base—from which to operate. This causes confusion and mixed messages, all of which leads to why the family is dysfunctional and needs my help in figuring out why they are having problems. You probably won't have to look far to see a family in a similar situation.

"We value you, but . . ."

The same thing happens in the corporate world. Let's take a company that professes to value its employees, saying they are the most important part of the business. Then the company experiences a sudden downturn in the economy. The company immediately lays off a third of its employees—at the same time giving raises to the corporate heads and/or stockholders. It's obvious the culture of the organization is unhealthy because its behaviors don't match its beliefs. The employees will interpret the leadership's behavior as flagrant disregard for employee needs. That will, in turn, lead to indifference on their part: "if the leadership doesn't care about us, why should we care about the organization?"

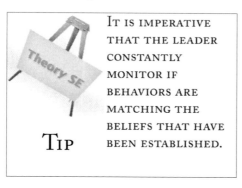

IT IS IMPERATIVE THAT THE LEADER CONSTANTLY MONITOR IF BEHAVIORS ARE MATCHING THE BELIEFS THAT HAVE BEEN ESTABLISHED.

TIP

There are times when a company cannot avoid to lay off workers. However, if a company is operating from a healthy culture, the company will seriously and conscientiously consider all options before making the decision to disrupt employees' lives by eliminating their jobs. In the hypothetical case above, the leaders could have opted to forego their raises and redirect that money into the employees' payroll fund. The leaders' behaviors would then have matched their beliefs, proving to the employees that the leaders did, indeed, value its workers as the most important part of the company.

Cultivating Culture

You might be wondering, "Is every failure due to an unhealthy culture?" The answer of course is NO. A business can fail for many reasons, just as a family can fall apart for many reasons. However, when analyzing the reason for failure—whether in family life or business—the first thing I examine is the behaviors and beliefs of all entities involved.

Examining behaviors and belief provides the same outcome for successful businesses as it does for families. If I were a betting man, I would bet you'd find a very healthy culture underlying each success. Beneath the healthy culture would be: 1) a sound belief structure that had been disseminated through the organization or family, and 2) a close match of the organizational/family behaviors to that belief system.

To expand on this, I would like to take some real-life examples of people we should all be familiar with from recent history.

It Depends on How You Define "Culture"

Former President Bill Clinton: When you look at the tripod model of leadership relative to the Clinton presidency, you can readily see that all the components of the tripod were in place— except the culture base, which was missing. Some would argue,

instead, that his ethic and moral brace was damaged or missing.
I disagree. He did have a set of ethics and morals, although they
may not have been the same as yours or mine. The problem was
with his culture. He espoused one set of beliefs to the American
people and to the people of other countries, but he behaved in
a much different manner. Thus, his credibility was undermined
and he lost focus and effectiveness as a leader. A presidency that
had many successes was overshadowed by the glaring inconsis-
tencies in his behavior from his espoused beliefs.

Jim Bakker: This successful television evangelist's story
closely parallels Mr. Clinton's. Like Clinton, charisma and success couldn't save him from disgrace. And it couldn't prevent the
entire PTL organization from falling apart. The obvious "dis-
connect" between his behaviors and beliefs eroded the culture
and resulted in a major personal and organizational collapse.

Any dysfunctional family: You probably know one or at least
have heard of one. Think about that family's patterns of behavior versus its beliefs. Are there incongruities? You might also
consider the shows you see on TV. Watch these shows with the
definition of culture in front of you and judge when the culture
described in the show is unhealthy.

A Balanced Life

There are also plenty of stories of successful families, organizations, and leaders. Here are some of my favorites:

Billy Graham: If ever a man "walked the talk," it is this great
man of God. For decades Billy Graham not only has made his
beliefs evident, but has yet to exhibit any behavior that does not
synchronize with his espoused beliefs. In everything I've heard
and read about him, I have learned that his life is a portrait in

consistency. Even though his crusades literally bring in millions of dollars, he has only taken a modest salary, making sure the rest goes back into his ministries. His behaviors match his beliefs!

Former Presidents Jimmy Carter and Harry Truman: While still in office, both of these presidents were maligned. Neither man was even expected to win the presidency. However, both,

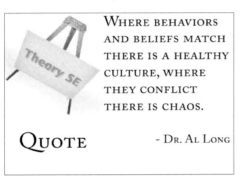

WHERE BEHAVIORS
AND BELIEFS MATCH
THERE IS A HEALTHY
CULTURE, WHERE
THEY CONFLICT
THERE IS CHAOS.

QUOTE   - DR. AL LONG

it seems to me, were men whose behaviors matched their beliefs. History is showing that both were effective leaders. I recently heard one historian characterize Jimmy Carter as the most intelligent president we have ever had. In the short term, some leaders may appear to be effective, yet eventually fail; however, in the long term, those who live a balanced life—a life in which behaviors match beliefs—will stand the test of time and leave a legacy as effective leaders.

George Huff: I have been blessed over the past thirty-five-plus years to be a part of the Huff family through marriage to my lovely wife, Carol. While I admire many in the Huff family, I am especially grateful to have known her father, the late George Huff. This family leader, whom I affectionately referred to as "Joe", always behaved in a manner that reflected what he believed. In all the years I knew Joe, I never saw anything in his behavior that contradicted his beliefs. His life was as amazingly consistent as Billy Graham's. He was giving, caring, and always put others before himself. Because he taught the same behaviors to his children, his legacy now lives on in our family and in the new families of our children. One man's balanced life has made a difference in countless lives.

Summary: A Firm Foundation

As we have seen, it takes more than a properly assembled tripod to ensure effective leadership. The tripod needs to rest on a firm base if it is to perform properly. That sound base is the culture, which is made up of the behaviors and beliefs of the leader, organization, or family unit. Keep that image of the tripod in your mind. It can have all the right components and be as strong as we can make it, but without a healthy culture to support it and keep it level, it could easily slip into the quicksand of failure.

Case Scenario

You are the leader of a local community action group try-ing to bring new families into your community. During one of the brainstorming and input sessions one member brings up the problem and reality that gangs operating in the community are becoming a serious problems that could negatively affect community growth.

One member of the committee stands up and says that he understands why gangs are growing in this community and states that kids join the gangs because it is a "healthy" culture. There is an outcry of negative response to his statement.

1. Do you agree with the statement "that kids join gangs because it is a healthy culture" after having read the chap-ter? If yes; why? If no; why?

2. How will you respond as the leader of the group?

3. What will be your first action step?

CHAPTER 7

INSIDE THE LEADER'S BRIEFCASE

A tripod is not an end in itself. The tripod's function is one of support. With that in mind, I've included a Leader's Briefcase alongside the model of the Leadership Tripod. In this briefcase are accessories that will both enhance leadership and improve the organization. The implements I am suggesting in this chapter are only a few of the many tools available to leadership. I hope you will feel free to add items as you see fit to enhance and improve

CONSTANTLY SEARCH FOR NEW TOOLS TO ADD TO YOUR LEADERSHIP BRIEF-CASE. NEVER BELIEVE YOU HAVE EVERYTHING YOU NEED. LOOK FOR WAYS TO CONTINUOUSLY IMPROVE.

TIP

your leadership. Of course, I hope you will share your information with me so that we can then share it with others who find the leadership tripod model useful.

The Telescope: Looking to the Future

Tripods and telescopes were meant for each other. On a starry night, or when some astronomical event is about to occur, we often see a telescope perched atop a tripod in someone's backyard. The telescope, of course, makes faraway things appear closer than they really are.

One item the leader can and should have at the top of the Tripod of Leadership is a *telescope*. Anyone in leadership can benefit from the telescope's ability to see things at a distance and bring them closer. Every organization needs someone to be looking toward the future. Many times the future is closer than we really think, but we always need to think in future-oriented terms. A future-oriented perspective helps us plan ahead and keeps leadership on its competitive toes, poised and ready for change.

Just as the astronomer uses a telescope to look for threatening asteroids, the leader needs to be alert for those things that might harm the organization. Just as the astronomer uses a telescope to look for answers to science's many questions, the leader looks to the future for ways to strengthen and diversify the organization as a whole. In the strategic planning module we discussed earlier, this telescope can be used to cast the vision for the organization and its leaders.

Putting Thought into It

Many planets are visible to the naked eye, but with a telescope, the astronomer can study planets with much more precision and see many more details. The same is true of the leader. Without taking the time to *THINK* about the future of leadership and the future of the organization, the leader and the organization operate without the full range of their capabilities. The leader must carefully study what is "out there" in the world, just as the astronomer studies what is "out there" in space. Failure to consider the whole picture limits the future of the organization to the here and now.

Visionary Thinking

The telescope of the leader is made up of two parts: time and mind. Leaders must take the time to think and must stretch their minds beyond their normal capacities.

The Ph.D. word for this kind of thinking is *metacognition;* i.e., thinking about thinking. Leaders must spend focused time using their minds as telescopes. This means looking to the future, troubleshooting options for growth, weighing possibilities, and anticipating what needs to be accomplished today to prepare for tomorrow. This activity is a prime example of Theory SE Leadership. The leader must be out in front of the organization, looking to the future and leading the organization down the path of success.

In the last two organizations I led, I tried to impress the leaders with the importance of *visionary* (telescope) *thinking.* I not only encouraged this kind of thinking, but I also challenged them to take time each day to *"THINK."* I told them that if they were not *thinking* in at least an uninterrupted thirty-minute time block each day, they were not doing the job I needed them to do.

The Microscope: Up Close and Personal

The next item on this abbreviated list of implements for the Tripod of Leadership is a *microscope.* Of course, the microscope is used to make smaller things look larger. With the microscope we are able to see organisms in minute detail that are not normally visible to the naked eye. The scientist finds this tool to be indispensable not only for identifying specimens, but also for analyzing the small details, both positive and negative, that might have a huge impact on the organism.

Know Your Sheep

The same can be said for effective leaders. They must know the organization they are leading in precise detail. This does *not* mean micromanagement. The flaw in micromanagement is that it fails to keep the "big picture" in focus and threatens to weaken rather than strengthen the organization. It focuses on the negatives and the "we can'ts".

Using a microscope approach means the leader has an intrinsic understanding of how the organization operates at all levels. This leader focuses on the positives and the "we cans", looking for mutually beneficial ways to edify and strengthen the organization. We could call this Theory SE Leadership and we could sum up its philosophy this way: "Know your sheep; know your flock."

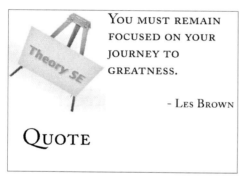

YOU MUST REMAIN FOCUSED ON YOUR JOURNEY TO GREATNESS.

- LES BROWN

QUOTE

The microscope is especially helpful when the leadership is creating the brace of strategic planning. It helps in evaluating an organization's competition, assessing the opportunities for cooperation, identifying organizational flaws, and highlighting organizational strengths. Careful analysis of the organization can help the leadership decide on ways to fix the problems they see under the microscope. Peering through this instrument also gives numerous opportunities to celebrate the organization's successes as well as finding small flaws before they become major problems.

The Camera: A Picture's Worth

The Leader's Briefcase contains the *telescope* to help leaders prepare for the future. It also contains the *microscope* to help leaders manage the details. Another tool in the leader's briefcase is the camera. It is the camera that can help leaders attain continuity in organizational planning. It is the camera that can help leaders relate or connect an organization's present state to its past. It is the camera that can help the leadership create and embrace its mission

Pointed at the Present

When first contemplating the *camera* on the *Leadership Tripod*, I thought of the snapshot as it captures a moment in the present. Being able to see what the organization is about at any given moment is important for all in the organization. This camera really captures the *mission* of the organization in the Strategic Plan Brace. What is the organization about today? How am I leading today? These are questions the camera can and should answer.

In the strategic planning process, this analysis helps the organization and the leaders drive stakes in the road to continuous improvement. As a leader you must have a handle on where you are today before you can plan where you are going tomorrow. *Otherwise, if you don't know where you are, how will you know where to go or even when you get there?* Leaders need to take snapshots of the organization and all its components to be sure they know where they are *now*.

Leaders also need to look at the organization from many different angles and through many lenses. .

A Look Back

The camera's uses obviously are not limited to the present. We must also remember the pictures we have taken in the past, the history of the organization and its leadership. When families get together for reunions, they often dig out the photograph albums. Looking at old pictures can jog our memories—helping us recall how things used to be, how far we've come, or how much we've changed.

The same is true in the organizational setting. Old pictures can help us remember how the organization has changed, what decisions prompted those changes, what decisions should have had more forethought. Effective leaders need to build on those snapshots, stressing their importance and urging the organization not to forget its history.

This historical perspective (the old snapshots) should not paralyze the organization and its leadership in a time warp of regret, so that the organization longs for things "to be like they used to be." That would be paramount to looking at old high school pictures and wishing we were as young and slim as we were then. *If we sit and ponder what once was for too long, we will never experience what might be.* Conversely, if we don't use our history to help us make informed decisions, we will be in danger of making catastrophic mistakes.

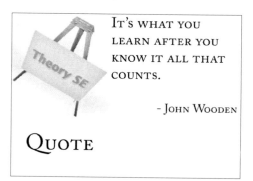

IT'S WHAT YOU LEARN AFTER YOU KNOW IT ALL THAT COUNTS.

- JOHN WOODEN

QUOTE

Photographing the Flock

The Theory SE leader would use the camera to take snapshots of his flock as a group, as they are in that moment of time. He would also photograph each sheep in the flock, taking note of any new lambs. He or she could then pull out pictures taken earlier and compare the old photos to the new ones. The new photos would clearly show how lambs had grown and matured. The old photos might also reveal a lamb or sheep missing from the new group photograph. This could be a valuable lesson in helping to determine why that sheep was no longer with the flock. If the sheep was lost because of a mistake, steps could then be taken to prevent such a mistake from occurring in the future.

The Transit: Establishing Boundaries

Of the instruments I have chosen to place on top of the *Tripod of Leadership*, this is one most people will seldom come across in their daily activities. Just because the *transit* is not found in the average toolbox does not diminish its importance. You see transits occasionally at construction sites or in areas that are being developed. One person will be peering through an instrument on a tripod. Some distance away, another person will be holding a stick with markings. These stick holders are using the transit to survey the land and establish boundaries.

Why does the effective leader or organization need to use a transit? Since you've come this far in the book, the answer should now be apparent. An organization and its leaders need to know the boundaries within which they will operate. When engineers finish their work with the transit, they submit a detailed report of their findings. The leader must do the same, making everyone aware of the organization's boundaries, the individual tasks to be completed within those boundaries, and the plan for the continuous improvement of the organization and everyone in it.

When positioned on the tripod, this instrument assists the leader in the *Responsibility* leg of leadership, as well as in *Authority* and *Accountability*. It also, in a macro sense, is used to complete the brace of *Strategic Planning*.

The Shepherd's Transit

The Theory SE leader would consider his transit to be a shepherd's staff. The "tool kit" of the eastern shepherd always includes a staff, which is used both as an offensive and defensive weapon. Comparing the transit to a staff in this case would be to highlight its use as an offensive tool: to keep the sheep in the flock. The shepherd sets boundaries on how far to let one of the flock stray. When a sheep wanders past those boundaries, the shepherd hooks the curved portion of the staff around the animal and gently pulls it back into the fold. Just as the shepherd needs to set boundaries and the sheep need to be aware of them, the leadership must also be aware of their boundaries. It's not a matter of "limiting" an organization or team member's potential. It's a matter of setting parameters and then framing them.

Summary: Tools that Enhance

In this chapter I have highlighted only a few of the many tools or instruments that could be used effectively on the Leadership Tripod. My hope, however, is that you will see how the model can spur thinking, encouraging all the stakeholders in an organization to think differently and using the model as a springboard for continuous improvement.

Always think in positive terms. For example, someone might decide to set a *laser* atop the tripod. True, a laser could be an efficient tool to pinpoint problems and slice out areas of which are not productive. It could also be used to micromanage or split apart the organization. Any additional tools added to the briefcase must be carefully examined to ensure they strengthen and not weaken the *Leadership Tripod*.

Self-Assessment Exercise

1. Are you a visionary thinker? What evidence would you give to support your answer?

2. How aware are you of the details of the organization you lead? What evidence would you give to support your answer?

3. If someone asked the question, "Where is your organization today?" How would you answer the question and what evidence would you give to support your answer?

4. How do the stakeholders you lead know what the organization's boundaries are and/or their specific positions within those boundaries?

5. What additional tools could you add to the leader's briefcase and how do you think they would strengthen the model?

Case Scenario

You have been contacted by a head hunter and asked to apply for a position of leadership in a company/organization in a state far from where you currently reside. You got through the interview process, study what you could find out about this privately owned facility and make the decision to take the job.

In your first few weeks, you quickly find out there are many problems in your new organization. There has been a revolving door of leaders as well as other stakeholders even though the company is financially sound.

1. What will you take from your leadership briefcase to place on your tripod and help you improve this leadership position?

2. Explain why these tools will aide you in your leadership activity.

CHAPTER 8

PALETTE OF
KNOWLEDGE

Palette of Knowledge

In this author's humble opinion, leadership is an **ART**. It is a talent one must continue to perfect, practice, and perform. Although some leaders may have more inborn skills and abilities to lead than others, that does not mean they are equipped for life. All leaders, whether novices or those with years of experience, need to continually build on their skill and knowledge base in order to continue experiencing success in leadership.

You might have already realized that in the previous chapter I left out one very recognizable use for the tripod—to support an artist's canvas. We call such a tripod an easel. The artist places a canvas on the easel to free his or her hands to hold the palette and paintbrush. The palette holds the individual colors into which the artist will dip the paintbrush, skillfully transferring those colors to the canvas.

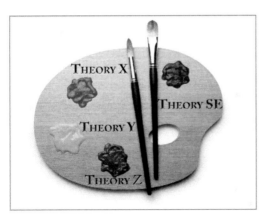

In the right combination and under the artist's watchful eye, paint and canvas will meet in a creative display of art.

Instead of thinking of a palette of colors, I would like the reader to think of this book as a Palette of Knowledge. The effective leader must take the colors of knowledge discussed in this book and paint them onto the canvas of leadership. When skillfully applied in the right proportions, these colors create a beautiful and worthwhile portrait of the effective leader.

The Right Mix

On this Palette of Knowledge are, of course, all the different *leadership theories*. If leaders are to create an accurate portrait of leadership, they must have all the colors (theories) of leadership at their disposal. Using only one theory would be like expecting the painter to use one color to create a portrait of someone. This portrait might resemble the person, but it would be one-dimensional, limiting the extent to which the artist could capture the individual's true likeness.

Likewise, if the painter used only primary colors and did not mix one with the other, the painting would be garish and unrealistic. By mixing colors, just as in mixing theories, the painter can capture the subtle nuances and idiosyncrasies that make each person unique. Using all the knowledge available to them, leaders can create leadership portraits that are distinctive, versatile, and applicable to a variety of situations.

The Right Support

This Palette of Knowledge works in conjunction with the easel, which is supported by the legs of *Authority, Accountability,* and *Responsibility*. All three legs must work together to hold the canvas at the proper angle. If the easel is off balance, the canvas may tumble to the ground, ruining the painting.

The braces of *Strategic Planning, Communication,* and *Ethics and Morals* contribute to the strength of the easel, ensuring the portrait can fulfill its destiny as a masterpiece.

The Right Foundation

If the artist is worrying that the easel might slip at any moment, he or she will not be focused on the primary task of painting. The artist may have to put down the palette and even the paintbrush occasionally in order to make adjustments to the easel. This causes an interruption in the flow of creative ideas.

We have learned from our study that the *Leadership Tripod* has to sit on a firm foundation if it is to function properly. This foundation or base is the *culture* of the organization, reinforced by the organization's *beliefs* and *behaviors*.

The artist's tripod or easel must also rest on a firm foundation. If the easel rests securely on a sound base, the artist will have more freedom to exercise the creative aspects of his or her craft. If the artist isn't worrying about whether the easel will hold the canvas, he or she will not be distracted and can tend to the many details of the painting. This includes tending to the craft of painting itself. An artist may have a picture in mind of what the completed painting will look like. To achieve that, he or she will not scoop up paint indiscriminately and start hurling it at the canvas. That would clearly demonstrate a disparity between beliefs and behaviors. The true artist follows a method, painstakingly working to apply the picture in his or her mind to the canvas. The true artist also hopes that each new painting will show improvement over the last.

The Right Tools

In addition to the easel, canvas, and palette, the artist needs special paintbrushes to create a portrait. These brushes are the tools in the *Briefcase of Leadership*. Just as the artist needs brushes of different sizes and types, the leader needs the Telescope, Microscope, Camera, and Transit. Each brush the artist uses has a specific purpose. Some of the tools create lines. Some tools are used to slather on great amounts of paint. Some tools are used to apply delicate pinpricks of color. All the tools contribute to making the individual elements of the portrait come together into a single work of art.

DON'T EVER LET YOUR PAINT DRY. AN EFFECTIVE LEADER WILL ALWAYS BE LEARNING AND ADDING PAINT TO HIS/HER PALLETTE.

TIP

The same is true with the tools in the briefcase. Each is used for a different purpose, but all are needed to ensure that the portrait of leadership is as complete and accurate as it can be.

My hope and prayer for you as a leader is that your canvas will portray the most accurate picture of leadership possible. An artist without a full Palette of Knowledge cannot complete the portrait. If you do not continue to add to your Palette, refilling and refreshing each color and adding new colors, your portrait will not attain its full potential. And that is what leadership is all about—being all you can be and helping others to do the same.

May you always lead with style and grace
And live your life at a balanced pace.
A palette of Knowledge is what you need
To paint the portrait of the way you lead.
May you cry a little, but laugh much more
Stay strong and healthy and let your spirit soar.

– Dr. Al Long

Theory 5E

CHAPTER 9

THE PAINTER

The Painter

We have gone through a study of why the *Leadership Tripod* is needed and the components of which it is comprised. Now we need to discuss the final piece, that of recruiting, selecting and retaining the most effective leader to be sure the *Leadership Tripod* is understood and implemented properly. To do this we will discuss each of the three phases both from the perspective of the decision maker and the prospective leader.

It should be evident why this section is so important, but to continue to use our parable of the painter, it would be like having a great tripod, at a great location, resting on solid ground, with a canvas in place on which to create a masterpiece. The plan is in place, with everyone knowing what is going to take place. The subject of the picture to be created has been decided upon. But, no one has selected the painter to actually paint the portrait.

The selection of the leader(s) is by far one of the most important decisions for any organization. To do an effective job of this most important process, it should be looked at very carefully and planned well. Likewise for the prospective leader, he/she should have carefully examined how and what the process will entail and should look at the process as interviewing the potential employer as much as the potential employer is interviewing the leader.

> **Tip**
>
> BE SURE TO TAKE THE TIME TO KNOW WHAT KIND OF LEADERSHIP QUALITIES YOU NEED IN A LEADER AND/OR IN AN ORGANIZATION YOU MAY BE ASKED TO LEAD.

Let us first look at the recruitment process. From the company point of view, it is my opinion that many organizations make errors at this crucial stage in searching for their leader. The first step any organization should take is to gather stakeholders (to whatever extent decision makers feel appropriate) and develop a detailed profile on the type of leader that is needed. Some of the issues which should be examined are;

1. The remaining leadership team
2. The strategic plan and the needs developed from it
3. Strengths and weaknesses of the former leader
4. Available resources

Once the needs assessment has been completed and a snapshot of the type leader needed is agreed to, then the search can commence. What I have seen, however is that many companies tend to do what they have always done and not look at new and innovative ways of deepening their pool of candidates. This can be done in several ways, and it is this author's opinion that it should be an eclectic approach. Using several different sources and methods will only make the chances of getting the best leader to fit the current needs of the organization more realistic and take the guess work out of the process. Just as one size fits all leadership theory is not good business, using only one source to generate leadership candidates can be just as damaging and limiting. Some of the more traditional methods are;

1. sending out notification of opening through trade magazines, placement bureaus, etc.
2. contracting with "head hunters"
3. networking with like companies
4. raiding competition
5. specifically targeting possible candidates

6. promoting and grooming leaders from within

From the prospective leader's viewpoint, the process of exploring and finding new leadership opportunities also is extremely important. Again, what many have done in the past is probably limiting to those who are anxious to lead. In the past, many leaders have followed only the more traditional routes to positions. Head hunters, placement announcements and bureaus are probably the most often used conduits for finding new positions. Of course these methods still exist and sometimes have great success but limiting their search to only these traditional methods may cause would-be leaders to miss a great opportunity to serve. These more traditional methods also come with an expensive price tag if a candidate enters into a contractual agreement with a placement service. The painter of today has to be more aggressive, spend appropriate time networking and use all methods available to find the right fit.

When counseling future leaders and those making a change, I encourage them to think of the search for a position as a long term process. Leaders should not to jump into a position from an emotional point of view, but spend time carefully analyzing what is best for their careers and what is best for the company. My counsel to them is to be passionate about leading, but patient in finding the right opportunity.

Once the pool of potential candidates is deep enough it is time to start the actual selection process. From the decision making body's perspective this can be done as simply or as complex as they desire. Typically, some sort of screening process for the initial round of candidates selected for interview would take place. Whether this is done with a large or small group of stakeholders is totally up to the organization and should reflect the current needs of the organization. Likewise, the organization needs to decide what process they will use, and how many leaders will be interviewed. They need to decide how many times prospective candidates will be interviewed before a final recommendation and offer is made.

Specific criteria need to be developed for use in judging whether or not this prospective leader should go on to the next round of interviews. This author also believes at this initial screening process, a set of "canned" questions should be scripted so that each potential candidate has the opportunity to react to exactly the same questions. Questioning each candidate with the same questions enables the interviewers to make a concrete comparison of the candidates. If this suggestion is not followed and different questions are asked of the various candidates, there is no way to be consistent in the analysis of the strengths each person could bring to the company.

I have come up with three different areas the candidates should be questioned on to enable the organization to select the best possible leader. Without looking at all three, it is not possible to accurately assess each candidate. The three areas that questions should concentrate on are **Head, Hands and Hearts.** What I mean by this is that questions should reflect the candidate's knowledge (head), their skill set (hands), and their hearts (feelings and emotions). Without concentration on and specific questions addressing each of these areas, it would be easy to have a mismatch between the leader and the organization.

Included after the Post-Assessment of the book are some sample questions and an accompanying rubric which will help quantify what normally is a very subjective process. This process will not and should not take all the subjectivity from the process, but it will give some concrete numbers to compare each of the areas.

Head:

It should be understandable why it is necessary to judge the knowledge base of the candidates. The candidate's knowledge of not just leadership, but of the company or organization as well as the knowledge of the industry should all be addressed. It should be important to the decision makers how the candidate stays current with the latest and best in leadership practice as well as what is going on currently in the industry. If an organization plans to stay ahead of its competition and work towards continuous improvement, how can it do so if the leader does not model that behavior? If a forward moving company hires a status quo leader, the company culture could be well on its way to imploding and the base of the tripod would quickly crumble.

Personally, I always like to ask candidates what they have read recently that has helped them be a better leader. I then like to ask what they have read personally for recreation. If they hesitate or can't answer the question, the answer to this question is a great way to separate those who take the Head part of their job seriously. An inventory of what the candidate has read demonstrates either an eagerness to learn more about their chosen field, or they may think they already have all the answers.

From the potential leader perspective, this question and answering quickly can help separate their candidacy from others. Even if an interviewing team does not ask the question, the candidate should find ways to work what he/she has recently read and learned into an answer to a question. This will demonstrate to the interviewer that at least the candidate is keeping up with the most recent developments in their area of expertise.

The decision makers and/or screening group as well as the potential leader should look for ways to differentiate candidates in the area of Head (knowledge). I know we have all said that we know people who are very intelligent, but don't seem to have common sense. The reality of the situation is that an effective leader needs to have both, but the Head knowledge is of paramount importance. Bringing in a leader with no knowledge of the company/organization and expecting them to have the respect of those they are leading is most assuredly going to be difficult at best and may be an impossible hurdle for an otherwise good leader to overcome.

Hands:

The Hands piece of my trilogy of selection tools is also very important. The areas of skill needs for each organization are going to differ, but the selection committee, as well as the potential leader, needs to be very clear on the base skill set the leader needs to be able to lead an organization. This skill set should be established early in the process by the decision makers and any stakeholders they choose to have involved, but it needs to be as complete as possible. If some of the traditional means to gather potential applicants are used as discussed earlier, these skills should be enumerated so both the organization and the candidates are clear about the base line skills needed.

Probably the first skill that comes to mind is technology. What level of technology is needed to effectively lead the organization? The technology skills will vary from organization to organization, but the candidate's level of expertise must be matched to the organization's needs. To exemplify the tragic consequences of not addressing this issue, I would like to discuss a real life experience that was shared with me.

A company was looking for a CFO. The position had outgrown the previous CFO and the owner of the company began to search for a replacement. The owner looked within his sphere of influence and looked at friends and acquaintances to fill the position. The owner casually mentioned his need for a CFO to a friend, who was a leader in a totally different industry. Both the owner and the friend became excited about the opportunity to work together, but they bypassed much of what has been discussed in this chapter in the interview process. First, the friend had no Head knowledge of the industry and it was quickly discovered that the friend did not have the Hands (skills) as well.

What was needed for the position was someone with accounting background and a thorough understanding of the accounting package the company was using. The friend had neither; the Hands (skills) were not present. What was tragic about this situation was that the friend (painter at the wrong tripod) left a position where he was highly successful and went to a position that lasted only a few weeks. Because of the lack of planning and forethought from both the owner and the friend, the owner had to find a new CFO, and his friend had to find a new job. This situation could surely have been avoided if the owner had taken more time to look to the Head knowledge and the Hands (skill set) of the friend.

However, the mismatch was not all the owner's fault. The friend too, should have thought of the Head and Hand knowledge needed rather than just letting emotions and ego rule his decision making process.

It is not to say that a leader or potential leader cannot gain the Head and Hand knowledge needed to successfully lead an organization with which they have had no experience, but that lack of knowledge and skills should be recognized up front and a process to address the weak areas should be in place before an agreement is ever reached between the two parties. A transition plan should be put into place with a specific timeline so all concerned will understand the process.

It should go without saying that the Hands (skill sets) go much deeper than just a potential leader's skill with technology. These skill areas could include such things as managing resources, constructing marketing materials, public speaking ability and a myriad of other skills. It is just important for the organization and the potential leader to have a thorough understanding of the skills needed to succeed.

Heart:

The final part, and perhaps the most important, is the Heart. What is meant here is what kind of person does the organization want and what kind of an organization from a Heart standpoint does the potential leader want to lead. In educational circles this is referred to as dispositions; how does one feel?

The decision maker and/or selection committee perspective they needs to know how the potential leader feels about issues that are important to the company. An example may be whether or not the candidate feels that people are more important than profit. One company may want a "bottom line" person, while another may want a people oriented person where the "bottom line'" is secondary to keeping valued employees. In either case if the leader feels one way and the company feels the other, and these dispositions are not discovered in the selection process, the potential match-up could be another wreck waiting to happen. If both parties understand how the other "feels" (Heart), there is much less chance of conflict in handling situations.

An effective way to get at the Heart issues in the interview and screening process is to use scenario type questions. The interviewer should ask the candidate about real life situations and have them react from the Heart as to how they would respond. Some candidates may try to answer the way they think the interviewer wants them to respond, so a series of these questions should be asked and by different interviewers, at different phases of the process. The interviewers can then compare answers to be sure the answers of the candidate are consistent.

From the candidate perspective, the interviewee should always "speak the truth" and let the interviewer or team know exactly who they are from the Heart standpoint. The interviewee should never try to out-think the questioner and should always be truthful and consistent in answering questions. The company and/or organization needs to know exactly who they are hiring from the Heart standpoint as well as the candidate's potential leadership ability. The idea of espousing one belief and then behaving differently once hired, is an example of how the *Leadership Tripod* will topple quickly as well as causing damage to the culture of the organization as a whole. If this happens the base of the *Leadership Tripod* is skewed quickly and the organization and the leadership will not be as strong and productive as it could and should be.

The final piece of this chapter is devoted to how to retain leadership and consistency in an organization. Although it is inevitable that leadership changes will happen, the more consistency in effective leadership that can be retained will equate to more dollars to the bottom line and the more chance for continued growth and prosperity. Notice I did say effective leadership. If there is an effective leader in place, the decision makers should do everything in their power to retain and reward that leader. Conversely, if the leadership is ineffective, the decision makers need to quickly change so as to not destroy the company. It is not fair to stakeholders or stockholders to allow an ineffective leader to continue in a position of leadership.

To retain the leadership an organization can look to two different reward systems; intrinsic and extrinsic. From my experience both are important and either can be more important based on the factors the effective leader and the organization are experiencing at any given time.

The most traditional and easiest way to reward is the extrinsic method. Many leaders are striving to receive a healthy raise, giving stock options, giving a bonus, and/or negotiating that "Golden Parachute". In no way do I want to discredit this as important, but some people can only spend so much money, take so many trips and sell only so much stock. These extrinsic rewards to leaders can also shatter the culture of the organization if the company happens to be in a downturn and staff has been cut, but yet the leader receives a healthy jump in compensation (extrinsic reward).

Some leaders need intrinsic rewards may be what they need to help the Heart of their leadership (attitudes). An extension of a contract, a letter of commendation, recognition at company meetings, or other non-monetary rewards may mean more to a leader than more compensation. I know some are reading this and questioning my sanity, but I know from personal experience that this is the case. I once heard that "money isn't everything, but it is right up there with breathing". I know that sufficient amounts of money are necessary to attract and keep good leaders, but the intrinsic rewards can be just as important.

The other day I was in a discussion about intrinsic versus extrinsic rewards when it came to rewarding a sales staff. Sales people are often motivated by monetary rewards. On the other hand, however, when the money is spent, there is nothing to show for their success or their contribution to building the company. My suggestion was that we need a combination of both kinds of rewards. I suggest that they be given them a monetary reward, but do so in front of their peers and along with some token of their achievement that would remain long after the money is spent. Such things as plaques, certificates of recognition, etc, can go a long way in helping motivate and retain all staff, including the leaders.

If you would permit me I would like to give a very personal example of the importance of intrinsic reward. It is a little different in the fact that the intrinsic reward was given to me upon my departure from a corporation, but it still exemplifies my point. I had been asked to leave my current leadership position and go to another. I had thought, prayed and examined carefully if I should make the move. The corporation I was serving had served me and my family well and had taken good care of us from the extrinsic perspective. They had also, on many occasions, given me the intrinsic rewards by word and action.

As many times happens, however, I felt called to take on the new role. Instead of being angry at me for leaving, my board invited to take my wife and me out to a farewell meal. We felt honored (intrinsic) that this group of individuals would want to do this for us. At the end of the meal, they presented me with a plaque that stated how much they appreciated my time serving them. That plaque still hangs proudly on my wall and each time I look at it, I feel affirmed and fondly remember the time spent serving that corporation. They could have given me money, but by now that money would be long gone. That award plaque will be hanging on my wall as long as I am here on earth and it will continue to reward me with the intrinsic feelings it evokes each time I look at it.

Of course there needs to be a balance of intrinsic and extrinsic rewards, but both are necessary. Each organization and each leader should look to both to help retain quality and consistent leadership.

Summary:

In this chapter we have discussed the recruitment, selection and retention of the leader from the leader's perspective as well as the decision maker's perspective. If an organization and/or leader does not concentrate on this most important aspect of leadership (being and/or selecting the best painter [leader]); the *Leadership Tripod* will not be as strong and effective as it can and should be. The process of planning before, during, and after selecting the leadership of an organization is of paramount importance to the overall effectiveness and profitability of the company.

Case Scenario

Company perspective:

You are a manufacturing company who has just lost your leader to a competitor. Your company is growing, but you are not seeing a corresponding growth to the bottom line in an increase in production and product development. Even with this growth, as far as gross profits, your net continues to decrease on a percentage basis and your stockholders are getting a bit nervous.

You have had a new product line in R and D for several years and it is just about ready to be launched. You and your stockholders are looking at this to jump start your profit margin and increase the value of your stock.

Leader perspective:

You are a very successful leader in a small manufacturing company. You have read recently that Company A has lost their leader to one of their competitors. Although very successful and satisfied with your present position, the idea of leading Company A is something you have thought of several times before. They are in the same type industry as you are, but have never reached the profits you believe they could.

Question set Company perspective:

1. What as a company will be your first step in searching for the new leader?

2. Develop a series of three questions; one from Head, Hands and Heart perspective.

3. How will you assess the answers?

Question set Leader perspective:

1. How will you go about getting into the process?

2. How will you differentiate yourself from other applicants?

3. What will you bring from the Head, Hands and Heart perspective?

One final note:

Readers can go on line at www.workingtogetherinc.com for sample interview questions, rubrics for scoring as well as tips for those interviewing and those being interviewed.

The Parable of the Would Be Artist Revisited

Our impetuous young man in the introductory parable wanted to be the great artist; like many want to be the great leader. Although we look at our young man and quickly judge his actions as unrealistic and without thought, many organizations and leaders make the same mistakes as our eager young friend in the forest.

We don't take the time to learn about leading and/or adequately equip ourselves and our organizations; just like our young man didn't take the time to properly equip himself for his artistic endeavors.

Sometimes we feel that anyone can lead; just like the young man felt anyone can paint. We feel the tools we have are good enough because they may resemble the tools some other leader or company has; just like the young man thought his tools resembled those of the great master. Our friend thought his tripod was good enough; his canvas was obtained by his own hand; his palette had been used before; and someone had at least opened his cans of paint. He even had a back up plan by taking his trusty camera with him in case the painting thing didn't work out.

Isn't it the same with some of us in leadership when we are satisfied with "just good enough" or resembling some other leaders or organizations and having that plan B in case other things don't work out?

Frankly, the young man was no artist and frankly we have many among us who are not leaders. Many want to short cut the process. They use an unsteady tripod with no firm base and no braces with the wrong tools or no tools at all and then are puzzled when the organization ends up in chaos or bankruptcy.

To be a master artist it takes time, effort, education and tools and of course talent. To be an effective leader it takes the same. Both vocations, I believe, are arts, and neither happens by accident and without hard work and dedication.

Appendix I

Sample Corporation
Strategic Plan

Vision

Sample Corporation will be a leader in construction quality and service to all clients. All those who deal with and are affected by Sample Corporation will know it as a company of honesty and integrity.

Mission

Sample Corporation partners with clients, subcontractors, and fellow employees in providing quality projects while establishing positive relationships and maintaining the highest level of integrity. As a team, Sample builds on experience leading to being more creative and efficient in meeting present and future needs of the community.

Goals/Objectives

We believe we are and need to continue to be financially stable.

1. We will examine and make appropriate changes in our bidding and cost estimating, as well as becoming more selective in our project selection process, by September 1.
2. We will establish target markets by June 1.
3. We will establish and implement a financial incentive program for all staff by April 1.

We believe we are and should continue to be a company of integrity and honesty.

1. We will revise the customer satisfaction survey to include feedback on integrity and honesty by August and fully implement the survey by October 1.
2. We will prepare and disseminate job descriptions for all staff.
3. We will develop an assessment process and review process for all staff by April 15. A part of this process will focus on integrity and honesty.

We believe in completing quality construction projects.

1. We will strive to have 100% of all contracts signed and delivered for all jobs before they begin by September 1.
2. We will compile subcontractor lists and differentiate them in categories by July 1.
3. We will formalize a system of assessment of subcontractors for site superintendents by June 1.

We believe marketing is a team effort.

1. We will establish target markets by June 1.
2. We will determine current market share by June 1.
3. We will obtain ten (10) new clients by April 1.
4. We will develop market ancillaries and distribute to all staff by June 1.
5. We will implement our Web site by September 1.

We believe in effective communication.

1. We will begin a weekly communication from Steve via E-mail by April 15.
2. We will establish monthly superintendent meetings by April 30.
3. We will conduct quarterly meetings with all staff.
4. We will conduct at least two social activities by April 1.

Appendix II

Personal Vision, Mission Statements
Personal/Professional Goals

Vision Statement:
I will leave this world with a legacy for those who follow and, above all things, be remembered as a "man of God."

Mission Statement:
In all things I do, I will attempt to approach each person or activity as a man of God. I will attempt to be a man of integrity and treat all those I deal with in a respectful manner. I will at all times attempt to be a solid Christian, a good husband, father, grandfather, friend, employee, and person.

Personal Goals and Objectives:

1. Be a better Christian.
   a. I will read a minimum of one chapter of the Bible per day.
   b. I will get more involved in church activities.
   c. I will continue to pray daily.
   d. I will continue my work with J. R. to try and get his time reduced.
   e. I will faithfully complete my duties as a member of the leadership council.
   f. I will finish my training for being a lay counselor.

2. Be a better Husband.
   a. I will do something special for my wife on a minimum of a weekly basis.

    b.   I will think of my wife's needs first.

    c.   I will help around the house without being asked.

    d.   I will go to camp with her if she is assigned.

3. Be a better Father.

    a.   I will be aware of my children's needs and help to meet them.

    b.   I will be available more for all my kids.

    c.   I will do something "special" with each or all.

    d.   I will be more positive and affirming in my relationships with my children.

4. Be a better Grandfather.

    a.   I will spend quality time with each of my grandchildren.

    b.   I will allow and celebrate their individual differences.

    c.   I will attend their activities.

5. Be a better Friend.

    a.   I will call my friends and/or write them notes of encouragement.

    b.   I will keep a log of my contacts with my friends.

    c.   I will cultivate and deepen relationships in our small group.

6. Be a better Person.

    a.   I will take better care of myself by losing weight.

    b.   I will exercise a minimum of three times per week for 30 minutes.

    c.   I will read recreationally at least six books through out the year and log those books.

d. I will increase my personal savings account by year's end.
e. I will spend less time watching TV and more time in developing relationships.

Professional Goals/Objectives:

1. Be a better Employee
    a. I will increase my expectations for all my students and grade them accordingly.
    b. I will attempt to find ways to help at the university to improve their teacher education programs.
    c. I will complete all consulting duties in a timely fashion.

POST-ASSESSMENT

Note to the reader: Please take this test after you have read the book.

1. In your organization, what is the level of knowledge in leadership theory and application?

2. How aware are you of others responsibilities?

3. Do the stakeholders have authority to clearly carry out their responsibilities?

4. Do you know how you are held accountable?

5. Is there a strategic plan in place for each group and is it clearly understood and used as a base of reference for all decisions?

6. How would you rate the communication lines within your organization?

7. How would you rate your ability to communicate?

8. Are your ethics and morals clearly indicated?

9. Is the culture (climate) of the organization healthy and do your behaviors and beliefs match that of the organization?

10. How important do you think the concept of leadership is to the success of your organization

11. What have you gained from reading Leadership Tripod? How will you put this knowledge into practice in your workplace, family, or any organization with which you are affiliated?

THE LEADERSHIP INTERVIEW INSTRUMENT (LII)

GENERAL CONCEPT

The following is a partial example of the Leadership Interview Instrument (LII) referred to in Chapter Nine (Page 182) of this text. For the full version of the instrument, please go to www.workingtogetherinc.com.

SECTIONS
Instrument divided into the following sections:

Head –   *Information possessed* by the candidate in *critical paths*

Hands –   *Abilities demonstrated* by the candidate that proves competency in *critical functions*

Heart –   *Attitudes, Behaviors, Beliefs and Values internalized* by the candidate that indicates temperament as well as potential actions and reactions to *critical situations*

Section			Questions
Head			What have you read professionally/ personally in the last…?
	Hands		What skills would you bring to the organization that differentiates you from other candidates?
	Hands	Heart	What causes you to want to be part of our organization?
		Heart	In your last position if we ask both your strongest supporter and your strongest adversary, what would they say about you?
Head			What type of leadership theory/style do you believe you operate from most often?
		Heart	When do you feel most energized in your work?
	Hands	Heart	What are your top (3) most recent accomplishments (that you're most proud of)?
Head			What do you know about our organization?
Head			What do you know about our competition?
Head	Hands		What do you know/what are your experiences with teams?
Head	Hands	Heart	Use SWOT technique to ask four-part question

SCORING

- Each interviewer should rate the candidate's response on a scale of 1-10 with 10 being the highest.